Freedom of
Conscience and
Religious Freedom

ALBA HOUSE
a division of St. Paul Publications
Staten Island, N.Y.

Freedom of Conscience and Religious Freedom

Louis Janssens

Translated by Brother Lorenzo, C.F.X.

WITH AN APPENDIX ON RELIGIOUS LIBERTY BY VATICAN COUNCIL II

First printing November 1965

Second printing January 1967

Nihil Obstat: John A. Goodwine, J.C.D., Censor Librorum
Imprimatur: Terence J. Cooke, V.G.
New York, N.Y. September 29, 1965

Library of Congress Catalog Card Number: 65-28503 ✓

Published originally by Desclee de Brouwer under the title
Liberté de conscience et liberté religieuse.

Designed, printed and bound in the U.S.A. by the Pauline Fathers
and Brothers of the Society of St. Paul at Staten Island, N.Y.
as a part of their communications apostolate.

CONTENTS

CHAPTER 1

THE TEACHING OF JOHN XXIII
AND OF PAUL VI

On September 29, 1963, on the occasion of the opening of the second session of the Second Vatican Council, His Holiness Paul VI devoted an important passage of his address to the subject of religious freedom: "What affliction to see that in certain countries religious freedom, just as some other fundamental rights of man, is suppressed because of principles and systems of political, racial, or religious intolerance! It is a profound sorrow to have to observe how many blows at the free and honest profession of personal religious faith are still perpetrated in the world." In the immediate context, within this passage, the Pope deplores the threats, harassments and restraints suffered by Catholics in countries where the Church is persecuted, and he asks that the members of the Catholic Church be looked upon as honest citizens and workers. Does it mean that he lays claim to religious liberty for Catholics alone? By no means. He clearly intends to proclaim a universal right. As a matter of fact, he presents religious freedom as one of the fundamental rights of man. Moreover, he defines it as "the free and upright profession of personal religious faith," and the adjective "personal" shows that it is a question of the religious faith to which one adheres personally, following the conviction of his conscience.

By placing religious freedom in the same category as that

of the fundamental rights of man and by implying that it arises from a conviction of one's personal conscience, Paul VI reaffirms the doctrine of his predecessor. Indeed, in his encyclical *Pacem in terris*, John XXIII places religious freedom among the number of universal, inviolable and inalienable rights which belong to every man because of his dignity as a human being. He stresses explicitly that it is an application of the duty of following the "right norm" (*ad rectam normam*) of one's personal conscience.[1]

Religious freedom is, therefore, a case of applying freedom of conscience, which is a matter of capital importance. But in what does true freedom of conscience consist? How must the *recta norma* of the personal conscience be explained, or, following the Italian text of the encyclical, *la retta coscienza*? The technical expressions used in the encyclical have their history. In order to understand their exact import, it is necessary to put them in the traditional context from which they came.

Now, concerning the *recta conscientia*, we have a double theological tradition.

First of all, there is the Thomistic tradition. In the terminology of St. Thomas the qualitative *rectus* designates the conformity to objective truth.

Conscience is right when its judgment is consistent with the objective requirements of the moral standard. St. Thomas always opposes right conscience to erroneous conscience. In this way he affirms that all conscience, whether it is right or erroneous, obliges,[2] although in different ways.[3] He distinguishes clearly between obligation of conscience and the objective morality of acts. On the one hand, an act can be obligatory in conscience while not being in conformity to the objective truth of the moral norm: "Secundum hoc enim ligare conscientia dicetur quod aliquis, nisi conscientiam impleat, peccatum incurrat, non autem hoc modo quod aliquis implens recte faciat." On the other hand, in the matter of the counsels, for example, an act may be objectively upright and not be obligatory in conscience: "Implens consilium *recte* agit sed tamen ad consilium dicimur non ligari." [4]

St. Thomas utilizes the term *ratio* to designate both the moral objective norm and the subjective norm which is the judgment of conscience.

He defines the objective norm by the following expressions: *secundum rationem esse,*[5] *convenire vel repugnare rationi,*[6] *ordini rationis,*[7] *ordini rationis ad finem cummunem (totius) vitae humanae,*[8] *rectae rationi.*[9] What does he mean by *recta ratio?* Reason is the rule of our will insofar as it reflects the eternal law [10] or, in a particular case, for example, God communicating a special order to Abraham or to Osee, when it is in conformity to the will of God: "Ratio hominis recta est secundum quod regulatur voluntate divina, quae est prima et summa regula: et ideo quod homo facit ex voluntate Dei, eius praecepto obediens, non est contra rationem rectam, quamvis videatur esse contra communem ordinem rationis." [11] In that way reason is the proximate rule of willed activity, the eternal law is its supreme rule, the act is righteous if it conforms to the order of reason and to the eternal law.[12] The rectitude of reason and that of the human act are therfore defined by the conformity to the requirements of the objective morality.

In the definition of the subjective norm which is the judgment of conscience, St. Thomas calls equally upon the term *ratio* — ratio vel conscientia [13]— in this sense that the conscience applies the rules of the *recta ratio* in actual situations.[14] But this *dictamen rationis* can be erroneous — *ratio vel conscientia errans* [15] — and, in this case, the will which obeys it is not right because it is not in conformity with the eternal law.[16] Therefore, the goodness (objective rectitude) of the human will is much more dependent on the eternal law than on human reason, to the extent that when human reason is in error one must have recourse to the eternal law.[17]

This Thomistic conception of the *rectitudo rationis, voluntatis et actus*, in the sense of conformity to the objective requirements of morality, equally dominates the definition of prudence insofar as it is *recta ratio agibilium*. The exercise of the virtue of prudence presupposes the rectitude or objective goodness of the will — *appetitus rectus est voluntas bona*.[18] That is to say, that in order to be able to act prudently, it is necessary beforehand to be well disposed with regard to the morally good ends of the actions, which presupposes the right judgment of these ends by reason.[19] It is then that the virtue of prudence intervenes in the acts which we place with the idea of realizing the morally good ends: it directs *ea quae sunt ad finem*. In other words, it assures in our acts the respect for the objective moral requirements which govern the realization of our good ends: it is the *recta ratio agibilium* and makes us act *secundum electionem rectam*.[20] This is why St. Thomas says that the truth of the goodness or the rectitude of the practical intelligence consists, according to Aristotle, in the truth corresponding to the right will, *verum conforme appetitui recto*.[21] Examining all the elements of our actions, he points to the objective requirements of morality: to be truly good the will must pursue an objectively upright end, grasped as such by an objectively true knowledge, and the act performed with a view to realizing this end will be objectively good only on condition that prudence introduces the requirements of the truth of the moral norm.

In the conception of St. Thomas (the source of Thomistic tradition, as Suarez[22] comments), *recta conscientia* is therefore clearly the conscience formed according to the demands of truth, of the moral objective norm. Certain passages of *Pacem in terris* also consider rectitude as the faithfulness of thought and action to the objective truth.[23] But is this also the case of the text which treats of religious liberty "ad rectam conscientiae suae normam"? If it were necessary to admit this interpretation, we would not understand why the Pope speaks of the personal conscience. Moreover, placing religious liberty in the category of personal rights, he indicates as basic, not the conformity of the judgment of conscience with the objective norms, but rather the dignity of the human person. Another explanation is therefore necessary.

Indeed, a second theological tradition exists concerning the *recta conscientia*, which, upon the testimony of Suarez,[24] comes from Duns Scotus. It was handed down and developed by the theologians of the Society of Jesus.[25]

While St. Thomas considers the rectitude of the practical judgment beginning with the rectitude of the antecedent will, Scotus makes a point of the rectitude of the subsequent will, enlightened by the practical judgment. Now according to him this judgment is practically true when the act of the will, judged upright, is in fact here and now subjectively upright, although perhaps it may not be so objectively, *quamvis fortasse secundum se non sit talis qualis iudicatur.*[26]

This conception of Scotus, Suarez has explicitly elaborated in his doctrine on the *recta conscientia*. The conscience can be true or erroneous in two ways: speculatively and practically. It is true speculatively, if its judgment corresponds to the objective requirements of the moral norm; it is true practically according to the particular situation of the subject. Suarez illustrates his doctrine by utilizing the episode told in Gen. 29:22-25 of which Jacob is the hero. Laban has given his daughter, Rachel, in marriage to Jacob and, on this occasion, he organizes a great feast. In the evening, unknown to Jacob, he brought Lia, his eldest daughter, into the bridal chamber. In all good faith the patriarch has relations with her. It is not until the next day that he discovers the fraud of his father-in-law. The judgment of conscience of Jacob, convinced of the lawfulness of his sexual relations with Lia, was true from a practical viewpoint taking into account the situation in which he was placed. But this judgment was speculatively false with regard to the objective reality: as in actual fact Lia was not the wife of Jacob. If, on the contrary, Jacob had considered that it was not his duty to satisfy the "rights" of Lia, his judgment would have been false from a practical viewpoint although speculatively true.

This coexistence of practical truth and speculative error is realized in the case of the conscience which is erroneous in an invincible way and, consequently, not culpable. In fact, in this case, the judgment of conscience is speculatively false, but true practically because the will consequent upon this judgment is right (*appetitus rectus*). In a similar situation, the truth of the judgment of conscience is called practical because there is real conformity with the will of the subject which, in a concrete situation, is truly right. In other terms, the practical truth of the judgment is not only a cognitive activity; it also functions as a causality. In fact, when speculative truth consists in the conformity with an object which it discovers, but which it does not constitute (*veritas speculativa non causat obiectum neque efficit ut sit ipsi conforme*), the judgment which is true practically exercises a real causality: it has as a result that the will which it informs is right. It proposes, as a matter of fact, the object in such a manner that the will follows it in a way that is right (*recte*). In that way the practical truth is not only knowledge (*cognoscitiva*), it is also practical, that is to say active and efficient (*causativa*). And Suarez concludes: "Ideo haec veritas practica non solum est cognoscitiva, sed etiam causativa atque ita quotiescumque appetitus, qui sequitur, honestus est, conscientia per quam regulatur vera est, et contrario, quandocumque conscientia est vera practice, appetitus qui ex illa sequitur, rectus erit et hoc modo recte dicitur veritas practica conscientiae sumi ex conformitate ad appetitum rectum, e contrario, falsitas practica sumitur ex difformitate ad eundem appetitum." [27]

The followers of this second theological tradition maintain therefore that invincible error, and, consequently nonculpable from the judgment of conscience, does not hinder the conscience from being right, from being *recta conscientia*. The object of our will being the known good, our will will be honest and right if in an invincible and nonculpable way we are convinced of following the moral good. And our will being honest or right, the judgment of conscience which guides it will also be practically, right or true, considering that the truth of the practical intelligence (according to the definition of Aristotle) is realized by the conformity with the right will, *veritas intellectus practici accipitur per conformitatem ad appetitum rectum*.

Let us emphasize that this conception of the uprightness of conscience although based on the dignity of the moral subject, as we shall see further on, is not subjectivist. On the contrary, it implies the realization of universally valid requirements.

First of all, not every erroneous conscience can be called right. Practical rectitude is accepted only in the case of invincible error, that is to say, when it is morally impossible for the subject to attain objective truth. In other words, rectitude of conscience presupposes the love of the truth, the sustained effort to promote the knowledge and appreciation of the objective good, so that the subjective goodness of the acts may better coincide with the requirements of the objective norms. As a matter of fact, the judgment of conscience is not in itself the supreme norm; it is only the indispensable condition for the absolute norm to be valid in fact for the subject which acts. Since the conscience decides the moral value of concrete acts not in virtue of itself but in virtue of the objective norms insofar as it is capable of grasping them, the obligation of searching assiduously for truth relative to moral acts is an essential condition of the *recta conscientia.*

But yet another condition exists. Granting that the practical truth of the judgment of conscience is defined by conformity with the right will, the formation of the *recta conscientia* requires that the will be right or honest. Now this right will consists in the love of moral good, in being disposed to taking to heart, always and in all things, the realization of what God wants from us in actual situations.

This fundamental choice, being a true act of the will and not a simple inclination, asserts itself by inciting the particular acts and in assuming their continuity by putting them in the service of the moral good. In other respects the unceasingly renewed effort to maintain the moral impetus of the particular acts confirms and intensifies the fundamental choice. The latter develops gradually as an acquired way of life. It affects the subject from now on. It is absorbed into its nature; in short, it acquires the firmness and constancy of a habit constantly capable of development, of a virtue. We can even say that the maintenance of the fundamental choice with respect to the moral good constitutes the development of *the* virtue, the various moral virtues finding their source in its dynamism by putting into concrete form its entire pursuit of moral good in the different domains of moral existence.

It is not surprising that Suarez, who considers the honest or right will as a basic element of the *recta conscientia,* concerns himself with this fundamental virtue. Twice he pauses over it.[28] An act of the will can be motivated by the love of moral good as such — *actus quo voluntas amat bonum absolute, vel bonum honestum ut sic'*[29] — its formal object can be moral goodness considered in itself and willed for itself — *objectum formale talium actuum esse ipsum generale motivum honestatis secundum se ac praecise sumptae.*[30] Such motivation suffices to give to the human act a proper and complete structure as a

moral act —"Est ergo ille actus in quadum propria et deter-
minata specie ultima actus honesti voluntatis, cuius objectum
formale est ratio honestatis ut sic, quatenus sumitur ut pro-
prium et particulare motivum, sub qua consideratione induit
rationem specifici obiecti formalis." [31]

If this act has its source in the dynamism of one virtue, it
cannot be the fruit of a particular virtue, such as temperance,
justice, etc., because the particular virtues direct us toward the
realization of particular aspects of moral good; it must therefore come from a special virtue — *a proprio et specifico habitu
sibi commensurato* [32] — whose formal object is the moral good
as such. This virtue, although it does not have any special
name,[33] is no less real. It is true that St. Thomas has not recognized the necessity of this virtue; for him the will is sufficiently
disposed and inclined to moral good as such.[34] But this
Thomistic conception of the will does not satisfy Suarez. In
fact, he said that the will is the dynamism of the whole man [35]
or of the spiritual soul which as such is the form of the body.[36]

It follows that the will, although inclined to the moral good
(to the requirements of the whole person as such), tends also
naturally towards particular goods such as the bodily goods
and pleasures. This variety of inclinations makes difficult for
us the effective pursuit of moral good as such, the realization
of which often requires the sacrifice of particular goods or
corporal pleasures. Now this difficulty of realizing the moral
good as a natural consequence of the diversity of the inclinations of the will makes necessary the maintenance of the love
of moral good, the development of a virtuous habit whose
formal object is *ipsum generale motivum honestatis secundum
se ac praecise sumptae*. Besides, the will is capable of acquiring
this virtuous habit, since it is also equally inclined toward
moral good and since the inclination can take root and become
a second nature thanks to acts in the service of this good. As
for the fecundity of this virtue, experience shows that the

acquired habit, which causes us to be inclined to moral good as such, contributes a great deal to developing a facility in the accomplishment of virtuous acts.[37]

Thus we can understand why in this second theological tradition the conscience can be called right even in the cases in which it is mistaken in good faith. Even then, the will is right or honest: the fundamental choice, the source of the particular act, is enlivened by the love of moral good. It is this love which also orders the search for the objective demands of the morality of the act: the judgment of conscience therefore has its beginning in the right will. Such a conscience is consequently sincere and right in its aim and, even if it is mistaken in good faith, its judgment suffices practically to assure the uprightness of the consequent will, since the good can be the object of the will only insofar as it is known.

Put in this perspective, the texts of Paul VI and of John XXIII concerning religious freedom, considered in the light of the conviction of conscience, take on a meaning of fundamental importance. We understand that, in order to safeguard the dignity of the human person, John XXIII proclaims the freedom of the private and public profession of religion *ad rectam conscientiae suae normam* if, even in the case of invincible ignorance, this rectitude implies the love of truth and the love of moral good or of what one believes to be the will of God. We see that Paul VI defines religious freedom as "the free and upright profession of personal religious faith," and the free involvement is upright when the aim of conscience is sincere and right and when the will is directed by a fundamental choice which is radically good.

---

1. "Every human being has the right to honor God according to the dictates of an upright conscience (*ad rectam conscientiae suae normam*), and the right to profess his religion privately and publicly. . . . And on this point Our predecessor of immortal memory, Leo XIII, declared: This

genuine, this honorable freedom of the sons of God, which most nobly protects the dignity of the human person, is greater than any violence or injustice; it has always been sought by the Church, and always most dear to her."

2. *Quodlib.* III, art. 27; *De Veritate,* q. 17, art. 3 et 4.

3. *In II Sen.,* d. 39, q. 3, art. 3; *De Ver.,* q. 17, art. 4.

4. *De Ver.,* q. 17, art. 4.

5. *Summa Theol.,* Ia-IIae, q. 18, art. 5; art. 8, ad 2.

6. *Summa Theol.,* Ia-IIae, q. 18, art. 5, ad 2.

7. *Summa Theol.,* Ia-IIae, q. 18, art. 8; q. 19, art. 1, ad 3.

8. *Summa Theol.,* Ia-IIae, q. 21, art. 2, ad 2.

9. *Summa Theol.,* Ia-IIae, q. 18, art. 9, ad 2: Nos autem hic dicimus malum *communiter* omne quod est *rationi rectae* repugnans.

10. *Summa Theol.,* Ia-IIae, q. 19, art. 4; q. 21, art. 1; q. 91, art. 2; q. 92, art. 2 et 3.

11. *Summa Theol.,* Ia-IIae, q. 154, art. 2, ad 2.

12. *Summa Theol.,* Ia-IIae, q. 21, art. 1: Quando ergo actus hominis procedit in finem secundum ordinem rationis et legis aeternae, tunc actus est rectus. Cf. Ia-IIae, q. 19, art. 4.

13. *Summa Theol.,* Ia-IIae, q. 19, art. 5.

14. *Summa Theol.,* Ia, q. 79, 13; Ia-IIae, q. 19, art. 5.

15. *Summa Theol.,* Ia-IIae, q. 19, art. 6.

16. *Summa Theol.,* Ia-IIae, q. 19, art. 6, ad 2: Ideo voluntas concordans rationi humanae non semper est recta sed nec semper est concordans legi aeternae.

17. *Summa Theol.,* Ia-IIae, q. 19, art. 4.

18. *Summa Theol.,* Ia-IIae, q. 19, art. 5, obi. 2: Appetitus autem rectus est voluntas bona.

19. *Summa Theol.,* Ia-IIae, q. 19, art. 3, ad 2.

20. *Summa Theol.,* Ia-IIae, q. 57, art. 5 Cf. *ibid.,* q. 47, art. 2.

21. *Summa Theol.,* Ia-IIae, q. 19, art. 3, obi. 2 et ad 2; q. 57, art. 5, ad 3.

22. F. Suarez, *Tractatus de bonitate et malitia humanorum actuum,* disp. 12, sect. 2, in *Opera Omnia* (éd. M. André, Paris, 1856), t. IV, p. 440, cites among the representatives of this tradition: Cajetan, Durand and Corduba.

23. For example, the encyclical speaks of the relations of Catholics with those "qui vel nullo modo vel non *recte* in Christum credunt," and admits that in historical movements, drawing inspiration from false principles, one can find positive elements, "quatenus videlicet cum *rectae* rationis praeceptis congruant."

24. F. Suarez, *Tr. de bon. et mal. hum. act., in Opera Omnia,* t. IV, p. 440.

25. Among the first to propose this were especially Suarez, Becanus (Martinus Schellekens), Lacroix, etc.

26. F. Suarez *Tr. de bon. et mal. hum. act.*, in *Opera Omnia*, t. IV, p. 440.

27. F. Suarez, *op. cit.*, p. 440-441.

28. F. Suarez, *Tr. de bon. et mal. hum. act.*, disp. 4, sect. 2. in *Opera Omnia*, t. IV, p. 322-323, and *Disputationes de virtute poenitentiae*, disp. 2, sect. 4, in *Opera Omina*, t. XXI, p. 37-40.

29. F. Suarez, *De poenit.*, disp. 2, sect. 4, in *Opera Omnia*, t. XXI, p. 36.

30. *Ibid.*, p. 39.

31. *Ibid.*, p. 37.

32. *Ibid.*, p. 37.

33. F. Suarez, *Tr. de bon. et mal. hum. act.*, disp 4, sect. I in *Opera Omnia*, t. IV, p. 323: Dico ergo hunc habitum esse specialem ab aliis distinctum, licet speciale nomen non sit ei impositum.

34. F. Suarez *ibid.*, p. 322, referring to *Quaest. disp. de virtutibus*, q. 9, art. 5, and q. 16, art. I, ad 7 and II, and to *In III Sent.*, dist. 27, q. 2, art. 3, ad 5.

35. F. Suarez, *Tr. de bon. et mal. hum. act.*, disp. 4, sect 1, dans *Opera Omnia*, t. IV, p. 323: "Sed mihi non est dubium quin his actibus (in quibus ratio honestatis praecise et propter se proponitur diligenda) correspondere possit aliquis habitus, quod in infusis est manifestum ... In acquisitis vero etiam existimo probabilius per hos actus acquiri habitum, quia non minus in hoc experientia ostendit quam in caeteris. Et ratio est quia etiam isti actus sunt difficiles, si efficaces sunt, et ex parte voluntatis est sufficiens capacitas et multiplex propensio et inclinatio, ratione cuius indiget habitibus: licet enim sit propensa ad honestum, habet etiam inclinationem ad delectabile et ad id quod est commodum corpori, quia est appetitus totius supositi. Et ideo veram existimo regulam quam constituit D. Thomas IIa-IIae, q. 17, art. 1, unicuique actui virtutis respondere bonum habitum."

36. F. Suarez, *Disp. de poenit.*, disp. 2,, sect. 4, dans *Opera Omnia*, t. XXI, p. 39: "Obiectum horum actuum (quorum obiectum formale est ipsum generale motivum honestatis, secundum se et praecise sumptae) per sese consideratum est difficile, nam respectu illius est quaedam repugnantia inclinationum et propensionum voluntatis. Ergo hoc satis est ut acquiratur habitus. Antecedens declaratur, nam licet in voluntate sit magna propensio naturalis ad honestum ut sic, tamen etiam est naturalis inclinatio ad bonum commodum et delectabile ipsi naturae et ipsi corpori. Nam cum anima rationalis ut sic sit forma corporis, ad ipsius commodum est propensa etiam per voluntatem, quae est proprius appetitus animae rationalis quatenus talis est. Ex hac autem inclinationum diversitate oriri solet difficultas in operando et inde etiam oritur necessitas aliarum virtu-

tum moralium. Unde probatur etiam prima consequentia, habitus bonus et virtutis circa obiectum bonum et difficile necessarius est... Sicut ex obiectis particularibus colligimus difficultatem obiecti specifici, ita etiam colligere possumus difficultatem obiecti in genere seu in maiori abstractione aut universalitate propositi. Atque ita bonum honestum ut sic difficile concipitur, non ex solis rationibus particularibus, sed ex hac communi quod repugnat aliquo modo sensui et inferiori naturae. Loquimur autem de bono honesto comparatione actus voluntatis efficacis et propositi absoluti exequendi illud."

CHAPTER 2

HISTORICAL ELEMENTS

During the nineteenth century the Magisterium of the Church was constantly preoccupied with liberalism and the "modern freedoms" it proclaimed. One may ask whether these interventions of the Magisterium brought a definitive solution to the problem of freedom of conscience?

In a fine study on the meaning of the various condemnations uttered by Gregory XVI, Pius IX, and Leo XIII, R. Aubert has shown that a good number of factors must be taken into account in order to understand the exact import of these pontifical documents.[1]

There are first of all the actual circumstances of the time: the liberal unrest against the temporal power of the Church, the fact that the systems inherited from the old order still remained in force in most Catholic countries whose people did not intend to deprive themselves deliberately of the considerable apostolic advantages which they thought they found in them, and the liberal stand for the total separation of Church and State. Above all, it is necessary to take into account the very way in which the problem of freedom was put at that time The popes condemned "that absolute and unbridled freedom,"[2] which springs from theoretical indifferentism, from naturalism and from rationalism. The situation was all the more serious because "the liberal Catholics of the nineteenth century, who

felt vaguely that there was legitimate and even Christian value
in certain claims of the modern conscience, were wrong in not
seeing the complexity of the problem and in claiming to make
rapid progress, since reconciliation of the Church — according
to a profound comment of Father Congar — with the world of
the day could not be brought about by introducing into the
Church some ideas which were accepted by the liberal world.
That would presuppose a profound change by which the permanent principles of Catholicism would take on a new development by assimilating, after having sifted and purified at
need, the valid contributions of this modern world." [3] Then
one understands the warning of Leo XIII: "It is necessary
to be careful not to be taken in by the specious uprightness
of these modern freedoms and to remember from what sources
they emanate and by what spirit they are spread and sup-
ported." [4] One, however, must not forget either that this doctrinal position does not include closing the door in practice to
all use of modern freedoms. "We agree to tolerate the rule
of modern freedoms in cases where we cannot avoid it and
on condition that the rights of the Church are safeguarded; we
are moreover in agreement in order that, where constitutional
freedoms have been imposed by public opinion, Catholics
may undertake the defense of religion and of the Church." [5]
Finally one must note that Leo XIII wrote that the Church is
not the enemy of a "sound and legitimate freedom," [6] and
that to freedom of conscience based on indifferentism he opposed true freedom which guarantees *honestissime* the dignity
of the human person: "If we understand by freedom of conscience the fact that each one can as he likes worship or not
worship God, the arguments which have been given above
are sufficient to refute it. But we can understand it also in
this way: that man has in the State the right to follow according to the awareness of his duty the will of God and of fulfilling His precepts without anyone being able to hinder him.

This genuine, this honorable freedom of the sons of God which most nobly protects the dignity of the human person, is greater than any violence or injustice; it has always been sought by the Church, and always most dear to her." [7] In this text and in other analogous passages, R. Aubert finds the beginning of a theology acceptable for freedom of conscience and he concludes: "Working on the wholly satisfactory elaboration of this theology, free from the philosophical postulates of doctrinal liberalism and of rationalism, constitutes one of the major tasks of current theology and it does not seem that, well understood, the documents of the ecclesiastical magisterium of the nineteenth cenury can constitute an insurmountable difficulty in the way." [8]

The wisdom of this conclusion, already proposed in 1951, is wonderfully confirmed by the passage, cited at the beginning of this study, of *Pacem in terris*, in which John XXIII, proclaiming freedom of conscience based on the dignity of the human person, refers explicitly to Leo XIII to reaffirm "the sound and legitimate freedom" that the pope opposed to freedom of conscience based on indifferentism. On the one hand, this passage of *Pacem in terris* excludes indifferentism and subjectivism, because it declares that religious freedom, in order to be legitimate, must have for norm a right conscience. But, on the other hand, in the theological tradition in which this passage is inserted, the rectitude of conscience is not impaired by invincible error and therefore is not culpable. From this point it seems that, to better set forth the foundations of this "sound and legitimate" freedom of conscience, guaranteeing *honestissime* the dignity of the human person, we must examine the most important elements of theological tradition concerning the erroneous conscience.

For this undertaking we take as a point of departure the *Glossa ordinaria*, as much *interlinearis* as *marginalis*. Recent studies attribute to Anselm of Laon (1117) and to his school a preponderant part in the elaboration of this gloss.[9] Whereas the first glosses were limited to interpreting the sense of scriptural texts, the ordinary gloss is preoccupied with the theological meaning of the glossed passages. For that purpose it is conceived as a vast compilation of Biblical commentaries inspired by the texts of the Fathers. Its authority was such that it was a companion-manual to the Bible and became in its turn the object of new interpretative glosses. It is especially Peter Lombard who played an important role as a propagator of the common gloss and, thenceforth, especially in the thirteenth century, it is considered as *auctoritas* by the theologians. The gloss *Pro altercatione* on the epistles of St. Paul, attributed to Anselm [10] himself, interprets Rom. 14:23 — *For all that is not from faith is sin.* The interlinear goss comments: "*Omne etiam bonum autem quod non est ex fide, quod fit contra fidem, id est contra conscientiam, ut credatur malum esse*, est peccatum." [11] This commentary establishes a clear distinction between objective morality and subjective morality. The subjective morality is presented as decisive in the sense that it is always a sin to act contrary to one's conscience. The marginal gloss adds an important detail: "*Non tamen omne quod fit cum fide bonum est, quia ignorantia quae est ex culpa nocet.*" [12] If it is unlawful to act contrary to one's conscience, it does not follow that every act conforming to a judgment of conscience is good, because culpable ignorance qualifies its goodness. This limitation clearly implies the distinction between culpable and non-culpable ignorance.[13]

Reflection on these assertions raises immediately several questions: From whence does conscience possess its strength of obligation? Why is it bad to act contrary to conscience, even if its erroneous judgment makes us transgress the law of God? When is error not culpable? In what fields of human activity can one admit the possibility of a non-culpable error? If the act following a non-cupable error is not a sin, can one affirm that it is morally good? It is with these questions that scholastic theologians were effectively concerned.

In his commentary on the Epistle to the Romans, Peter Abelard, who had studied under Anselm of Laon (1108-1113), took up certain of these questions when he explained *Rom.* 14:23: *Omne autem, quod non ex fide est, peccatum est.*[14] Following the commentary on this point he incessantly repeats that all that is contrary to conscience is sinful.[15] The reason is that God, who judges the intention, considers the objective reality of acts less than the preceding disposition.[16] Nevertheless, the problem must be examined more closely. Abelard takes as an example the case in which a real crime is considered as a good action by the conscience. Christ had said to His disciples: "The hour is coming for everyone who kills you to think that he is offering worship to God" (John 16:2). Consequently did those who killed some believers whom they considered seducers and therefore deserving of death commit a sin? If they had spared them, they would have acted contrary to their conscience and thus they would have sinned. But two questions arise. The first — if in fact they kill some innocent people, even some elect of God, which is an iniquitous act, will we dare to say that they do not sin or that in this action their purpose (*intentio* in the sense of plan which they wish to accomplish) is good, when in reality it proceeds from the greatest error and that, consequently, it is good only in their estimation, without being so actually? [17] The second — how does ignorance excuse them from sin, if it is true that one speaks of sins of ignorance? Does not the psalmist speak of the wrath of God in regard to the people who ignore Him (Ps. 78:6), and did not Our Lord implore the pardon of the Father for His executioners who knew not what they were doing (Luke 23:34)?

Would pardon be necessary if there had not been any fault? If, in fact, ignorance or even error concerning the faith excused from all sin, why would the Jews, the Gentiles, or other infidels be condemned for their unbelief when they think that their faith is right and that they would not persevere in a belief which they considered erroneous? It is, nevertheless, concerning them that Truth says: "He who does not believe is already judged" (John 3:18). Abelard is content with asking these questions. But he looks forward to discussing them in his *Ethica*.[18]

In fact, in this work Abelard takes up the same questions again and in the same order.

First of all, he affirms that the judgment of a conscience is an essential element of sin, that is, it must be mentioned in the very definition of sin. For Abelard, sin is a defiance of God, and to scorn God is either not doing for Him what we believe is our duty to fulfill or not omitting for Him what we believe we ought to omit.[19] There can be no sin where there is no guilt, and the latter can affect us only according to the judgment of conscience which we place on the malice of our free undertaking.[20] The role and the importance of conscience are therefore explicitly recognized in the very definition of sin as consent to what the conviction of conscience judges to be truly sinful in the eyes of God. If Abelard considers the opposition or rupture between the free engagement and the judgment of conscience as a constitutive element of sin, we understand that he admits, with the gloss, that acting contrary to conscience is always a sin.[21]

But if it is always bad to act against a conviction of conscience, does it not ensure that following conscience always makes the act good and meritorious? In order to stress this problem more sharply, Abelard goes back again to the example of the persecutors convinced that in martyring the faithful they are performing an act pleasing to God, according to the prophecy of Jesus: "The hour is coming for everyone who kills you to think that he is offering worship to God" (John 16:2). He mentions first of all the opinion of those who think that the design or plan is good and right each time that they *believe* that they are acting well and doing what is pleasing to God.[22] But the words of St. Paul raise an objection to it: "For I bear them witness that they have zeal for God, but not according to knowledge" (Rom. 10.10). Assuredly in this text the Apostle shows that he understands the ignorance of those who, in good faith, follow an erroneous conscience; he recognizes in them a great fervor and a desire to do what they believe is pleasing to God. But since they are mistaken in their zeal, their purpose (*intentio*) is erroneous, the eye of their heart is not sufficiently simple to see clearly, that is, to take precautions against error. Our Lord Himself makes a distinction between the rectitude or error of the plan that one is prepared to accomplish (Luke 11:34-35): if the eye is sound, that is, if the purpose is right all the acts which proceed from it will be sound, that is good.[23] And Abelard concludes: to be good it does not suffice that the purpose or intention be considered as good; it is also necessary that it be good in fact; in other words, it is not enough to believe that the term of our aim (that which we wish to achieve) is pleasing to God; it is still necessary that our judgment of conscience not be erroneous.[24] Otherwise, the unbelievers also would perform good and meritorious actions because, just as we do, they believe themselves to be saved or pleasing to God by their acts.

Is it necessary to affirm from this that, if it is not good or meritorious, the act placed in consequence of an erroneous conscience is a sin? To answer this question Abelard distinguishes between sin properly so-called and sin in the broad sense of the word.[25] Adequately defined sin is a defiance of God, and to spurn God is to consent to what we *believe* to be disorderly in the eyes of God. Consequently, we cannot commit sin when we are doing what our conscience judges pleasing to God. Moreover, there is no sin without guilt, and one is not guilty before God when one does not use one's freedom contrary to one's conscience.[26] By following a judgment of an erroneous conscience we commit no sin, except if the error is due to blameworthy negligence,[27] if the ignorance itself must be attributed to a sin.[28] All that is done by invincible ignorance [29] is not sin in the proper sense of the word and not blameworthy.[30] By way of examples Abelard cites the case of children and the mentally defective incapable of moral judgment,[31] the case of the infidels who do not believe in Christ because He has not been preached to them,[32] and the case of the executioners of Christ and of the martyrs convinced of doing what God expected of them,[33] etc.

Nevertheless, in all these cases we can speak of sin in the improper sense of the word inasmuch as the action, being judged as good, really is not: *peccati vocabulum large accipientes, illa etiam vocamus peccata quaecumque non convenienter facimus,*[34] *quod nos facere minime convenit, quod non oportet.*[35] Abelard cites as an example the sin of ignorance: "Tale est ergo (that is sin in the broad sense of the term) per ignorantiam peccare, non culpam in hoc habere, sed quod nobis non convenit facere, vel peccare in cogitatione, hoc est, voluntate (in the sense of spontaneous and indeliberate impulsion) quod nos velle minime convenit vel, in locutione aut in operatione, loqui nos vel agere quod non oportet, etsi per ignorantiam nobis invitus illud eveniat." [36] Sin in the broad sense consists then in doing, without any guilt, what is actually (objectively) contrary to what God expects of us, whereas sin properly so-called implies a contempt of God as we are guilty of the break between our assent and our judgment of conscience (*per culpam peccare, in consensu peccare, consentire in eo in quod credit consentiendum non esse*). Thus the executioners, convinced in conscience of the obligation of persecuting Christ and His disciples in order to be pleasing to God, committed a sin in the broad sense, while they would have committed a sin properly so-called (*gravius per culpam peccassent*) if they had spared them by thus going contrary to the conviction of their conscience.[37]

A final question remains which Abelard had put in his commentary on *Rom.* 14:23. If ignorance or error, even concerning faith, can excuse from all sin properly so-called, how can we interpret the words of Christ according to which the one who does not believe is already condemned? The unbeliever is not necessarily a sinner in the real sense. If it is not due to a fault of negligence — *nos proprie peccatum illud solum dici arbitramur, quod in culpa negligentiae consistit* [38] — that is, if it arises from ignorance or invincible error, it is only improperly called a sin; implying no fault, it is only a sin of ignorance — *non per malitiam, sed per ignorantiam*: [39] "Cum autem dicimus nos ignoranter peccare, hoc est, tale quid quod non convenit facere, *peccare* non in contemptu, sed in operatione sumimus . . . Si ergo isto modo peccatum dicamus, omne quod vitiose agimus, vel contra salutem nostram habemus, utique et infidelitas et ignorantia eorum quae ad salutem credi necesse est, peccata dicemus, quamvis ibi nullus Dei contemptus videatur. Proprie tamen peccatum illud dici arbitror, quod nusquam sine culpa contingere potest. Ignorare vero Deum, vel non ei credere, vel opera ipsa quae non recte fiunt, multis sine culpa possunt accidere. Si quis enim Evangelio vel Christo non credit, quia praedicatio ad ipsum non pervenerit, iuxta illud apostoli: *Quomodo credent ei, quem non audierunt? quomodo autem audient sine praedicante? (Rom.* 10:14), *quae hinc ei culpa potest assignari, quod non credit?"* [40] But, even non-culpable ignorance excludes from salvation: "Ad damnationem quippe sufficit Evangelio non credere, Christum ignorare, sacramenta Ecclesiae non suscipere, quamvis hoc non per malitiam, quam per ignorantiam fiat. Di qualibus et Veritas ait: *Qui non credit, iam iudicatus est (Joh.* 3:18). Et apostolus: *Et qui ignorat*, inquit, *ignorabitur (J Cor.*

14:28)." [41] In order to justify this frightening affirmation, Abelard finds no other way out than to recognize that the number of God's judgments are like an abyss whose depths we are unable to probe. [42]

With respect to the problem which concerns us, we can sum up the position of Abelard in four points: (1) Acting contrary to one's conscience is always a sin, considering that the judgment of conscience enters as a constitutive element in the very definition of sin. (2) Following an erroneous conscience in good faith is not a sin properly so-called, as in this case the ignorance is not culpable and there is no error through negligence. (3) Nevertheless, in this last case, the act is not good or meritorious because the term of the will's aim is really not suitable to us. Here Abelard is aware of deviating from another opinion which holds that the intention is good and right each time that in conscience one considers that he is doing what is pleasing to God, an opinion appearing to rest on the marginal gloss following which only culpable error harms the goodness of the act. (4) Unbelief, even due to invincible ignorance or a nonculpable error, excludes from salvation. Here again Abelard appears more strict than another author of the school of Anselm of Laon for whom the application of the phrase is limited to vincible ignorance and, consequently, culpable ignorance alone: "*Ignorans ignorabitur. Sic est intelligendum. Ignorantia necessariorum, id est sine quibus non est salus, si evenit per superbiam vel negligentiam damnat, aliter enim non nocet.*" [43]

The Franciscan teachers of the thirteenth century [44] reacted against the introduction of the judgment of conscience in the very definition of sin. The point of departure of their teaching is the definition of St. Augustine: *peccatum est dictum vel factum vel concupitum contra legem Dei.* [45] In this definition they insist on the objective malice of sin by emphasizing its opposition to the law of God. But they are equally aware of the passage of the gloss according to which all that is done against conscience, although it may be good in itself, is sin.[46] How then can the requirements of the objective moral order be safeguarded?

Their characteristic contribution consists in utilizing a distinction already initiated in the twelfth century between the different categories of acts.

Certain acts are intrinsically good, such as the act of faith or of charity.[47] Others are essentially bad, so fornication can never become lawful.[48] Conscience does not oblige when it forbids what is essentially good or when it recommends what is bad in itself. In fact, it must submit to the precepts and authority of God, according to the words of St. Paul: *Non est potestas nisi a Deo* (Rom. 13:1). In these cases it is sinning rather than following one's conscience. Moreover the gloss confirms that it is also a sin of acting contrary to one's conscience. Would it be a case of a puzzled conscience? No, it is only a question of an apparent perplexity: one must, in fact, free oneself from the error and escape in that way the bond and power of the conscience.[49]

Apart from some acts intrinsically good or bad, there are some indifferent acts, for example, eating and drinking.[50] In this area, conscience obliges — when, for example, it suggests that some food is poisoned — as long as we do not succeed in changing its erroneous judgment.

The pre-eminence of the requirements of objective morality is such that the role of conscience becomes secondary, indeed, negative. The conscience is capable of tearing down, not of building up. It can increase the sin, not lessen it. If we judge in conscience that an indifferent act or a venial sin is a mortal sin, we commit a mortal sin. On the contrary, a mortal sin. considered as venial, remains no less mortal.[51] It likewise follows as a matter of course that, to be good and meritorious, it does not suffice that an act be judged so by the conscience; it is necessary that it really be good and meritorious.[52]

Let us note that the Franciscan tradition is aware of another opinion according to which the conscience, even an erroneous one, obliges in all the categories of the act, at least *secundum quid*, that is, as long as it persists (*manente conscientia*).[53] In fact, the author of an anonymous question, while affirming that, according to the *communis opinio*, conscience does not oblige in every area, seems even to make allusion to the definition which Abelard gave of sin: "Ad illud quod quaeritur unde habet conscientia quod liget, dicunt illi qui ponunt conscientiam in omnibus ligare, quod hoc est quia tenemur voluntatem nostram voluntati divinae conformare quando *credimus esse* voluntatem." [54]

The secular masters [55] endeavored to scrutinize more the reasons and the limits of the obligation of conscience.

Abelard taught that in the sin the contempt of God consists in going contrary to the conviction of conscience. It is from this definition of sin and other considerations that the author of an anonymous question [56] asks if conscience always obliges. He answers by distinguishing.

Conscience always obliges in this sense that one can never act contrary to its judgment. In this case the gravity of the sin depends on this judgment of conscience: the sin will be mortal or venial according as the action placed is judged mortal or venial. From this point of view, the obligation of conscience is of natural law: "Ius naturale est scriptum in corde cuiuslibet ne faciat quod credit esse contra Deum vel quod credit non faciendum, quod idem est." It rests, moreover, on a scripture proof: "All that is not from faith is sin" (Rom. 14:23).

But if it is never allowed to act contrary to conscience whether it is true or erroneous, it does not follow that one is obliged to follow its judgment. Indeed, experience having shown that conscience can be deceived, one must not do immediately what it dictates, for fear that being guided by a blind man you may fall into a pit. It is necessary first of all to arrive at certitude and, to that end, we have at our disposal the light of faith, of synderesis and authority.

Gauthier of Chateau-Thierry [57] is especially concerned with the problem of the obligation of conscience: utrum conscientia liget, utrum conscientia erronea liget.

He dwells first of all on the point of view that conscience is always binding. However, if it is in error, it only obliges temporarily and accidentally as long as it persists and, because it is in error, it can and must be reformed.

He states the position of the Franciscan school in the same way: conscience exerts no power over good or bad acts in themselves; it can create an obligation only in the sphere of indifferent acts. He aligns himself with a third solution. Conscience does not oblige by itself (*per se*). It has obligatory force only in virtue of something else. In fact, what binds is the natural law or the commandment of God. The conscience only has to dictate and convey the obligation. As the judge is obliged to execute his sentence, not because it is his, but because it applies the law, thus conscience obliges only in virtue of the objective law and is consequent upon it. In other words, it is not the cause of the obligation but its sine qua non condition: no one, in fact, can know that he is bound to something by virtue of a precept of God if it is not through the medium of the judgment of his conscience. Knowing the law and on the basis of it, conscience points out and expresses the obligation.

As for the erroneous conscience, one must take into account that it is at one and the same time conscience and erroneous.

Insofar as it is erroneous and unable to rely on any precept in order to propose an obligation, it has to be reformed. It does not bind because it is mistaken and opposed to God. By following it, we perform an act bad in itself. Thus the executioners, following their erroneous conscience, committed a sin by crucifying Christ.

But as far as *conscience* is concerned, as long as it lasts, the erroneous conscience binds *ex consequenti* and *per aliud* in the manner of the right conscience, because in virtue of a precept of God it dictates the placing or the omitting of an act. Strictly speaking, it does not propose a real precept, but it is convinced that it is doing so. This would be, then, spurning God and, consequently, sinning rather than acting contrary to its judgment. Thus the executioners, by sparing Christ and by going in this way contrary to the judgment of their conscience, would have sinned.

If this is so, is not the erroneous conscience necessarily perplexed? No, because the perplexity renders the sin ineluctable *(est enim perplexitas quando est ad peccatum necessitas)*, while in the case of the erroneous conscience the error can and must be extirpated.

It is into the context of this theological tradition that we must place the problems again that St. Thomas considers and try to appreciate his contribution to their solution.

As far back as his Commentary on the Sentences [58] he endeavors to throw light on the obligatory value of conscience. The proper object of the will is not the good in itself but the good insofar as it is known. In other words, as long as it is not known, the moral law cannot even reach our will and direct our acts. It follows that the obligation which a precept of God imposes on us can "bind" *(ligat)* us only to the extent of the knowledge that we have of it. Therefore, we can conclude that the obligatory value of this knowledge is the same as that of the precept: the precept can "bind" us only through the medium of the knowledge that we have of it and this can oblige us only in virtue of the precept. Now conscience is nothing else but the application of knowledge to an act. It "binds" us then; it obliges us by virtue of the divine precept.[59]

We ourselves are not the authors of the laws which bind us, but it is by our act of knowledge that we are obliged to observe the laws made by others.[60]

This conception explains very rigorously how the cognitive aspect enters into the very definition of the proper object of the will. But does it suffice as an adequate expression of the obligatory value of the conscience? Is not the latter *nihil aliud quam applicatio notitiae ad actum?*[61] Gauthier of Bruges,[62] not without reason, it seems, reacted immediately against this very narrow conception of conscience. He recognized that, as knowledge and promulgation of the moral law, the conscience is only the condition sine qua non of obligation. But it is not restricted to communicating the obligation of the moral law; it has its own virtue, being itself a law of our moral life. In that way it brings into relief the nature of the moral law. Now the law presents various aspects. It implies at first a sort of pact in the sense that one will be rewarded or punished according to how we observe it or transgress it. The same holds true for the conscience. The law is also an order and, similarly, the conscience is a commandment in which the authority of the synderesis and of right reason is made valid. Law is also a habit which inclines action; conscience, too, takes on the fullness of an acquired habit in proportion as, by the fidelity that we employ in forming our judgments of conscience, we acquire the firmness and facility of judging exactly the moral requirements. These are invaluable comments for better determining the status of conscience.

St. Thomas has the great merit of having studied together and in their reciprocal connection the problem of conscience and that of ignorance and error, especially in two consecutive articles of his treatise on human acts.[63]

In the first, he wonders if the will, at variance with erroneous reason, is bad or, what he considers as the same thing, if erroneous conscience is binding. He builds up his answer by refuting the Franciscan School. According to this opinion, erroneous conscience does not oblige in the area of what is intrinsically good or bad in itself, and, in these matters, the will which deviates from it is not bad. It is only concerning things which are indifferent in themselves that erroneous conscience is binding, and the will which does not obey it commits a sin. St. Thomas replies that the object of the will is not the good in itself, but the good insofar as it is known. It follows that the will acts badly each time that it indulges in something which reason presents as an evil. Thus, to believe in Christ is in itself good and necessary for salvation, but if reason proposes it as an evil, the will would act badly in adhering to it. Not that it is a question of a thing bad in itself, but accidentally because of reason which represents it in that way. Therefore, it is necessary to conclude purely and simply that every time the will goes contrary to conscience, true or false, it is bad. This conclusion is confirmed by Rom. 14:23: *"Omne quod non est ex fide, peccatum est, id est, omne quod est contra conscientiam."* [64] Therefore, if the erroneous conscience proposes something which in itself is good, bad or indifferent as an order of God, then to scorn the judgment of conscience and the precept of God is one and the same thing.[65]

In the following article St. Thomas considers whether the will which obeys erroneous reason is good. He begins by saying that this question is identical with the question of knowing if an erroneous conscience excuses. For him, the answer depends on the nature of the ignorance, the source of error, and its relationship with the act placed. Ignorance can be voluntary either directly, and that is the case with deliberate ignorance, or indirectly, when one does not actually pay attention to what one would be able and ought to know and consider or when, by willful negligence, one is not desirous of acquiring the knowledge that one should have. If the error has its source in one of these forms of willful ignorance, the will complying with the erroneous conscience will be bad. It is the culpability of what is done because of being ignorant of what one can and ought to know that the Apostle has in mind when he writes: *Si quis ignoret, ignorabitur* (*J Cor.* 14:28). But there is also involuntary ignorance, antecedent to the will and which, as such, is the cause of acts which one would not will otherwise. This is the case of invincible ignorance. Error resulting from this invincible ignorance and, consequently not culpable, makes the act involuntary. Therefore, this error excuses from all fault a will which corresponds to an erroneous conscience.[66]

This statement raises two questions. The first — if, in the case of invincible ignorance, the will consequent upon an erroneous conscience is not bad, can one say that it is good? Does the act placed in these conditions meet the demands requisite for being good and meritorious?

In the article that we have just examined St. Thomas is concerned only with the conditions and requirements of objective morality. In the body of the article he shows that invincible ignorance renders the act involuntary (*causat involuntarium*). Now an involuntary act is not a human act. Therefore, it does not arise from the moral order and, in this connection, the question of moral good or evil does not even come up: "Manifestum est quod illa ignorantia quae causat involuntarium, tollit *rationem* et boni et mali *moralis.*" In the answers to the objections it is equally a question only of the requirements of objective morality. St. Thomas considers the conditions of an objectively good will: to be right the will must be in conformity not only with the conscience but also with the eternal law and the term of its purpose and its interest or its object must be in conformity not only with the judgment of conscience but also with the objective norm.

In the case of invincible ignorance, how does it stand in regard to subjective morality? If this ignorance is involuntary, it remains no less true that the act placed is voluntary from another point of view. It is a free attitude in relation to the moral modality which the conscience thinks it discovers in it. From the point of view of subjective morality, it will therefore necessarily be virtuous or harmful, affected with merit or with sin. St. Thomas writes in this connection: "Omnis autem actus humanus habet rationem *peccati* vel *meriti* in quantum est voluntarius. Obiectum autem voluntatis secundum propriam rationem est bonum apprehensum; et ideo actus humanus iudicatur *virtuosus* vel *vitiosus* secundum bonum apprehensum in quod per se voluntas fertur, et non secundum materiale obiectum actus." [67] In the continuation of the article he deals only with questions in which subjectively it is a question of sins. It does not impede the principle which he has just stated from not implying this restriction.

Faithful to his conception of the rectitude of conscience and of will, Suarez accepts all the consequences of this principle. First of all, in the case of invincible ignorance, being true and certain from a practical viewpoint, although speculatively erroneous, conscience is actually obligatory. *Formally* it binds, not to evil, but to good. Of course, the act which is placed will be materially bad, but this denomination affects it only as a material object, not as a human act. Similarly one can say that this conscience does not impose an obligation contrary to the law of God, but that it obliges to an act of virtue. Materially the action will be contrary to the law of God, but under the circumstances the latter does not bind because one is excused by ignorance and *by another more pressing divine law, imposing obedience with respect to the prudently formed conscience.* Moreover, the act conforming to this conscience is good and arises from the virtue that in good faith one thinks he is practicing. Indeed, conscience being true from a practical viewpoint, the will conforming to it is right.[68]

A second question remains: in what areas can we speak of

invincible ignorance? In other words, in what matters is error in good faith possible?

In a general way St. Thomas asserts that lack of knowledge is a sin for the one who can and ought to have it: "Scientia carere peccatum est ei qui potest et tenetur habere." Invariably he reaffirms that we must have knowledge which is indispensable in the performance of our duty, and that this requirement extends to three fields, namely — faith, moral law, and the duties of one's state in life: "Unde omnes tenentur scire communiter ea quae sunt fidei et universalia iuris praecepta, singuli vero ea quae ad eorum statum vel officium spectant." [69]

First of all, everyone is bound to know the duties of his state in life: "Unusquisque ... tenetur scire quae ad suum officium pertinent, sicut episcopus ae quae pertinent ad officium episcopale et sacerdos ea quae pertinent ad officium sacerdotale, et sic de aliis; et horum ignorantia non est sine culpa." [70]

Next, all those who have the use of reason are obliged to know the requirements of the moral life: "Unicuique peccatum est ignorantia eorum quae ad bonos mores pertinent." To what degree is ignorance necessarily culpable in this sphere? St. Thomas answers that the first principles of the natural law can and must be known by all men having the use of reason, and that ignorance in this domain is inexcusable, whereas various causes can impede the knowledge of precepts more remote from the first principles. Concerning the specific examples which he contributes, it appears that he allows no excuse for ignorance concerning the unlawfulness of adultery, while he does not exclude the possibility of error on the subject of the indissolubility of marriage, the prohibition of divorce, the malice of fornication, the moral quality of an oath and of personal prosecution. [71] Actually, he insists that all know the Ten Commandments: "Omnis homo tenetur scire praecepta decalogi, per quae potest peccata vitare et bonum facere." [72]

In fact, the Decalogue contains the first elements of the law, available to the knowledge of all. That is why God made it known to all the people, while He called upon Moses and Aaron to teach the more difficult things for which simple people need the enlightenment of the wise.[73] Moreover, all the commandments of the Decalogue can be reduced to the twofold precept of love of God and neighbor, and these two precepts are precisely the first and fundamental precepts of the natural law, attainable in itself by human knowledge either by the intellect or through faith: "Illa duo pracepta sunt prima et communia praecepta legis naturae, quae sunt per se nota rationi humanae, vel per naturam, vel per gratiam." [74]

In the main we can say that the content of the natural law is what becomes evident as worthy of man, as promoting the development of man as a human person. Man is an incarnate spirit provided with a conscience which is at one and the same time an intentional conscience and conscious of itself. The intentionality of our conscious existence entails that we are essentially open to the objects of this world, implicated in some relationships with other people, engaged with others in social groups, and, in all that, in harmony with God, and that our dynamic reality can develop only by assuming and by elaborating these relationships. In the dynamism of our conscious existence there appears a cognitive aspect, the intelligence, which directs us in an unbiased way toward the truth; in other words, it pursues reality in order to disclose it such as it is, and it submits necessarily to the truth perceived. It is therefore what makes us suited to discover what our behavior must be in our relations with the world, with others, with social groups, with God. So we can say that the content of the natural law or of the rational norm of morality is *what according to our unbiased thinking or according to the requirements of truth, actually and intrinsically is befitting to the human person adequately considered, that is, in his relations with the*

world, with others, with social groups, with God and with itself
in as much as it is conscious interiorness embodied in the
corporality.

If our knowledge takes on an absolute character, in as much
as it is essentially orientated toward reality in order to reveal
it such as it is, it is not, however, absolute in the sense that it
is always partial and, consequently, limited, susceptible to
growth and constant improvement. In fact, not to break away
from the reality with which it lives, it must keep itself in the
wake and dependence of experience, of authentic contact with
reality. Now, this experience inserts itself into a social context
and, in each moment of history, it is conditioned by the level
of objective culture (especially the sciences concerning man
and social relations: economics, sociology, ethnology, psychology, medical sciences, history, etc.) and the subjective
culture already realized (especially in the domain of knowledge, of affectivity, of the moral sense).

When the patriarchs practiced polygamy they were living
according to the requirements of moral values such as were
accessible to their knowledge. The cultural situation at that
time did not yet make it possible for them to see that polygamy
does not fit in with the objective norms ruling the coexistence
of man and woman. Suppose in our present-day civilization
that someone took it into his head to reintroduce polygamy
into the social order. We would protest against this flagrant
violation of the natural law. It is because our civilization lets us
set a much higher evaluation on the personal dignity of women,
appreciation for which the advent of Christianity has been
decisive, proclaiming the dignity of every human person,
whether free or slave, man or woman [75] — and by making
clearer the moral implications.

The requirements of human perfection come to light only
gradually. There is historical progress in the entrance into
awareness of moral values. It was necessary that humanity be

confronted with the fact of the existence of countries in the process of development and of the enormous economic possibilities of other nations in order for them to awaken to the consciousness — as John XXIII so admirably expressed it in *Mater et Magistra* — of the moral demands of this situation. There was a time when, in the relationship between employers and workers, the moralists were considering in practice only the question of a just wage. Since then hygiene has become a science, and its applications to the organization of an enterprise are of such a nature as to protect the health of the workers.

It is immediately evident that this cultural progress includes possibilities whose fulfillment constitutes a genuine advancement for the human person. Consequently, it is necessary to hail as moral progress the intervening legislation whose provisions are designed to assure better hygienic conditions in various enterprises; also, they have humanized more fully the relations between employers and workers. Technical development is an important aspect of cultural progress. It is clear that the constantly increasing technical possibilities take on a deeply human signification as long as people keep them in the service of man. But the utilization of technique presents some dangers: we understand that the legal stipulations relating to safety measures with the purpose of protecting the workers makes the relations between employers and workers more moral. Formerly, the workers generally very little educated, were merely the unthinking executors of the work ordered from above. At the present time, thanks to the democratization of education — one of the most favorable aspects of cultural progress — they are more and more competent and, by that very fact, capable of grasping the methods of production in which their work places them, of taking personal initiatives, of assuming wider responsibilities, of understanding the primacy of their work over capital, etc. It is no less evident that these new realities impose moral requirements: in an enterprise authority will have to adapt itself to them not only by conducting itself according to the principle of subsidiarity, but also by giving an active *participation* to the workers, according to their actual capacities, in the same direction. This simple example is instructive. All cultural progress offers new possibilities of promoting the dignity and development of men as human persons. It is by becoming rooted in experience, in the realistic contact with each new cultural acquisition, that the awareness and the knowledge of moral values to be realized from these possibilities must be deepened and enriched. The awareness of the requirements of human perfection or of the content of the natural law is an historic process. It expands with cultural progress which conditions it and which, in its turn, it must direct toward this development of human dignity.

The possibilities of human perfection are inexhaustible and each cultural acquisition presents possibilities, formerly unforeseeable, for human or moral advancement. Therefore, the natural law or the rational norm of morality asserts itself as an *objective, normative, never-failing* ideal.

The objective and normative character of the natural law implies that what is already known of it asserts itself with an intrinsic evidence and by that very fact is universally valid. It is what assures the continuity in the increasing specific knowledge of moral requirements. What is once acquired continues by existing in the new principles, but it will be integrated into a richer synthesis and will play in it a more accurate and more delicately expressed role. Let us give an example. The theology of the Middle Ages, faithful to the Augustinian tradition, considered the conjugal act only as an *actus naturae*, that is, as an act exclusively in the service of procreation. Saint Albert the Great was the first to discern in it the dignity of an *actus hominis*, that is, an act which has a personal meaning as an expression of love in the intersubjective relationship of the married couple. In our days, owing to a better understanding of the meaning of corporality in interpersonal relation, we see better and better that the sexual act is truly a conjugal act as it embodies the union of definitive and exclusive love between a man and a woman which is fulfilled precisely by marriage. The procreative sense of the sexual act, at least at the moments in which a conception is possible, remains no less real and essential for it. But it takes place in a more ample and complete synthesis and, hence, its human and moral signification is enriched. In other words, we no longer place side by side procreation and conjugal love as two separate ends. We throw a light on their intrinsic relationship. Indeed, the child is the *fruit* of conjugal love. First of all, he is born by an act which has as its intrinsic sense of being the expression of this conjugal love: the will for union, inherent in the love of husband and wife, becomes *concrete reality* in the child. The child is, moreover, the fruit of conjugal love because the latter is the origin of the collaboration of the couple in his upbringing. Therefore, we see better why the sexual act is on the human level a *conjugal* act: it incarnates conjugal love, and only the permanent community of life and love of the husband and wife is able to assure the educative formation of the child. This example shows very well the continuity and progress in becoming aware of the content of the natural law. The importance of procreation, emphasized in past tradition, is not diminished by the new acquisition; on the contrary, it takes on a more human and therefore more moral meaning in a wider and more complete synthesis.

But the natural law is not only constituted by objective norms, it is an inexhaustible ideal as well. As cultural progress continually unfolds new possibilities, man will never be at the end of his researches on the requirements of human perfection implied in these constantly increased possibilities. It would be a lack of humility and consequently of truth to think that we have exhausted all the riches of moral values. Our specific knowledge of moral norms takes its point of departure in the authentic contact which our culture of today allows us with reality. Does not cultural experience, conditioned by our culture and therefore limited, neglect certain human values and certain aspects of the true hierarchy? Does it not exaggerate certain elements at the expense of others being left in the background? Does not the peculiarity of our situation place an obstacle to learning certain requirements of perfection and of human dignity, requirements whose importance and values we do not even suspect? History which reveals the laborious progress of passed generations gives us every reason to believe that future generations will have to continually advance their consciousness of the content of the natural law, and that they will devote historical studies to our shortcomings and our deficiencies in our progress towards the development of man in his dignity as a human person. If this is so, invincible ignorance in the domain of natural law has as its fundamental reason the very historicity of our existence. The margin of ignorance on this level, as much for an individual as for a group, will depend fundamentally on the level of objective and subjective culture already acquired.

Let us add that, under Alexander VIII, a decree of the Holy Office condemned the Jansenist affirmation, according to which, in our condition after the fall, invincible error with regard to natural law did not excuse from formal sin.[76]

Finally, a third domain exists in which, according to St. Thomas, ignorance is inexcusable. It is that of the truths of the faith. In fact, if we are obliged to have knowledge of the truths which we need in order to accomplish our duty, in order to imprint a right orientation upon our acts, we are in like manner obliged to know the truths of the faith, seeing that it must direct the intention in our action: "Omnis homo tenetur scire ea quae fidei sunt, quia fides intentionem dirigit." [77] That is why all have to know the essential truths of Christian revelation, expressed in the Creed. Although the word of the Gospel has spread practically everywhere, it may happen that some people as a natural consequence of their isolation in the middle of the forest, have not received the preaching of the Gospel. Is their unbelief inexcusable? If they become receptive to grace, in His mercy God will help them by sending them a missionary, as formerly He sent Peter to Cornelius, or by enlightening them with an interior illumination. If they do not attain the knowledge of the essential truths of faith, it is because this help has not been granted to them as a natural consequence of previous sins, namely, original sin and personal sins and, therefore, they will be justly condemned for these sins.[78] In order to understand this severe position, we must take into account the historical development and the theological context: St. Thomas depends on a tradition strongly influenced by certain very rigid theories of St. Augustine and, his geographical horizon being very limited, he considered as fulfilled the words of the psalm (Ps. 19:5), used again only by St. Paul (Rom. 10:18): "The utterance fills every land, the message reaches the ends of the world." [79]

Since then, we have become much more realistic according as we have been confronted with the existence of great multitudes of men belonging to non-Christian religions, even with the fact of atheism. Who would dare to say that in such a situation ignorance of Christ and of His revelation would necessarily be a sin? The Church has rejected the assertion according to which "infidelitas pure negativa in his quibus Christus non est praedicatus, peccatum est." [80] It is not astonishing that theologians are always concerned with so fundamental a problem. Nowadays the interest in ecumenism communicates to it a fresh outburst of current interest. May it suffice to raise again some basic ideas, touching directly on our subject and dominating more and more current thought.

1. Holy Scripture attests that God wishes the salvation of

all men (I Tim. 2:4) and that this salvation, which is supernatural because of participation in the life of divine charity (Rom. 5:5) is communicated only by Christ, the Lamb of God who takes away the sins of the world (John 1:29) and the sole Mediator who has given Himself as ransom for us (I Tim. 2:6).

2. These scriptural facts imply that, from God's point of view all men are destined to the life of grace and that, from the point of view of men, all are actually in this supernatural order, either according to the mode of acceptance or according to the mode of refusal.[81]

3. Who would dare to think that this gift of grace which God destines for all men, would clash with the personal refusal of most men? While it does not justify this pessimism concerning men, the Gospel sets forth some decisive reasons for justifying our optimism, that is to say, our hope with respect to God: Since the Word was made flesh for us and died because of sin, who would be bold enough to maintain that, because of the refusal of men, the fate of the world and of humanity would follow the same course as in the hypothesis in which Christ would not have come? [82]

4. Anyone, even if he considers himself an atheist, who chooses in his life the fulfillment of moral good for the love of this good, chooses God, the supreme Good and the source of all good. His fundamental choice, made efficacious by grace, establishes his acceptance of the supernatural communion with God, although this dynamism may remain unconscious in him and although God is already, in some way, found and possessed without his having an explicit awareness of it.[83]

5. As a social being, man will live his relationship to God in the concrete religion that his environment communicates to him. In spite of his deficiencies and his errors, this religion includes some positive elements through which God promotes the salvation of those who adhere to it.[84]

6. Since the redemption that God decreed is the redemption by Christ and as there is only salvation in Christ, all those who share in the life of grace — in the gratia Christi — belong to Christ and, even if they profess another religion, they can therefore already be considered under certain aspects as Christians without the name.[85]

7. It does not follow that the missionary preaching of the Church could be considered as superfluous, under the pretext that, without it, one can already be a Christian in a certain way and without knowing it. To deduce such a consequence would be equivalent to concluding that, considering that faith and contrition are requisite for the fruitful reception of Baptism and Penance, one would no longer have to be concerned with these sacraments. The apostolic mission of the Church endeavors to make latent Christianity as fully conscious as possible, because Christ wishes the communication of grace through the social structure of His visible Church, and because the life of the Church assures the complete participation in the gifts of God. It is not by arrogance that Christians consider all sanctification as a gift coming from Christ and aspiring to its fulfillment in the Church of Christ; on the contrary, it is a requirement of their humble and docile submission to God, revealing His redemptive will in Christ and through the Church.[86]

Paul VI has resolutely placed himself in this current of thought, when in his opening discourse at the second session of the Council he said: "The Catholic Church looks farther, beyond the horizon of Christianity. How could she put limits to her love if she must make her love that of God the Father, Who showers His graces on all men (Matt. 5:48), and Who loved the world to the point of giving His Son for it? (John 3:16). The Church therefore spreads her concern beyond her own sphere. She esteems other religions which keep the sense and notion of one God, supreme and transcendent, creator and provident. These religions give worship to God by acts of sincere piety, and they set upon their beliefs and their practices the bases of the moral and social life. The Catholic Church calls attention, no doubt, not without sadness, to some gaps, some insufficiencies, and some errors in many of these religious forms. But she does not fail to turn towards them and recall to them that Catholicism esteems, as it must, all that they possess which is true, good and human."

It goes without saying that this historical insight furnishes us with a large number of elements directly concerning the problem of freedom of conscience and its most important application which is religious freedom. It is from this data we shall endeavor to examine the subject.

---

1. R. Aubert, *L' enseignement du magistère ecclésiastique au XIXe siècle sur le libéralisme*, in *Tolérance et communauté humaine*, Tournai, 1951, p. 75-103.

2. Gregory XVI, *Mirari vos*.

3. R. Aubert, *op. cit.*, p. 102.

4. Leo XIIII, *Immortale Dei*.

5. R. Aubert, *op. cit.*, p. 80.

6. Leo XIII, *Immortale Dei*.

7. Leo XIII, *Libertas*.

8. R. Aubert, *op. cit.*, p. 103.

9. Smalley, *The Study of the Bible in the Middle Ages*, second edition, New York, 1952.

10. O. Lottin, *Nouveaux fragments théologiques de l'école d'Anselme de Laon*, in *Rech. théol. anc. med.*, t. 14, 1947, pp. 159-160.

11. *Glossa interlinearis* (Lyon, 1950, t. VI, col. 178).

12. *Glossa marginalis* (PL, t. 114, col. 516).

13. In the school of Laon, they already distinguish *ignorantia invincibilis* and *vincibilis*. Cf. R. Blomme, *La doctrine du péché dans les écoles théologiques de la première partie du XIIe siècle*, Gembloux, 1958, p. 66 (note 3) and 84 (notes 1 and 2).

14. P. Abaelardus, *Exposito in epist. Pauli ad Rom.*, cap. XIV (PL, t. 178, col. 959).

15. *Ibid.*, col. 953-959.

16. *Ibid.*, col. 959: Deus enim qui cordis inspector est, non tam quae sunt quam quo animo fiunt attendit.

17. *Ibid.*, col. 959.
18. *Ibid.*, col. 959.
19. P. Abaelardus, *Ethica seu liber dictus Scito teipsum*, PL, t. 178, col. 636, 639, 653, 654.
20. *Ibid.*, col. 656, 654.
21. *Exp. in ep. ad Rom.*, col. 953-959.
22. *Ethica*, col. 652: Sunt autem qui bonam vel rectam intentionem esse arbitrantur, quotiescumque se aliquis bene agere credit et Deo placere id quod facit.
23. *Ibid.*, col. 653.
24. *Ibid.*, col. 653: Non est itaque intentio bona dicenda, quia bona videtur, sed insuper quia talis est sicut existimatur; cum videlicet illud ad quod tendit, si Deo placere credit, in hac insuper existimatione sua nequaquam fallatur.
25. *Ibid.*, col. 653.
26. *Ibid.*, col. 656, 657.
27. *Ibid.*, col. 657: Nos tamen proprie peccatum illud solum dici arbitramur, quod in culpa negligentiae consistit, nec in aliquibus esse potest, cuiuscumque sint aetatis, quin ex hoc damnari mereantur.
28. *Ibid.*, col. 653: Si talium ignorantia peccato minime est ascribenda. . . .
29. *Ibid.*, col. 657: vel quidquid per ignorantiam invincibilem fit. . . .
30. *Ibid.*, col. 653.
31. *Ibid.*, col. 654.
32. *Ibid.*, col. 653, 657.
33. *Ibid.*, col. 652-653.
34. *Ibid.*, col. 658.
35. *Ibid.*, col. 657.
36. *Ibid.*, col. 657.
37. *Ibid.*, col. 657.
38. *Ibid.*, col. 657.
39. *Ibid.*, col. 656.
40. *Ibid.*, col. 656.
41. *Ibid.*, col. 656.
42. *Ibid.*, col. 656-657.
43. *Setentia* nᵒ 141, in Lottin, *Psychologie et morale aux XIIᵉ et XIIIᵉ siécles*, t. V, Gembloux, 1959.
44. Cf. the edition of the texts in O. Lottin, *Psychologie et morale aux XIIᵉ et XIIIᵉ siècles*, t. II, *Problèmes de morale*, Iᵉ partie, Gembloux, 1948, p. 354-374.
45. An Anonymous Question in *Toulouse* 738, published by O. Lottin, *op. cit.*, p. 356, and attributed by him to Alexander of Halès; Jean de la Rochelle, *Summa de vitiis*, in O. Lottin, *op. cit.*, p. 359; an Anonymous Question in *Paris nat. lat.* 14726 in O. Lottin, *op. cit.*, p.

363; an Anonymous Question in *Vat. lat.* 781, in O. Lottin, *op. cit.*, p. 368.

46. Cf. the texts cited in the preceding footnote.

47. In the documents cited, we find successively the following expressions: Quaedum sunt determinate bona quae, prout huiusmodi sunt, non possunt male fieri (O. Lottin, *op. cit.*, p. 356); quaedum sunt formata, quae numquam possunt fieri malo fine (*ibid.*, p. 360); sunt quaedum bona per se quae secundum se formata sunt (*ibid.*, p. 362). S. Bonaventure, *In II Sent.*, d. 39, a. 1, q. 3, uses a broader expression: quae sunt secundum legem.

48. Here are the expressions used: quaedam determinate mala quae nullo modo possunt bene fieri (O. Lottin, *op. cit.*, p. 356); quaedam deformata sunt malitia culpae in quantum huiusmodi non possunt fieri bono fine (*ibid.*, p. 360); quaedam mala secundum se quae deformitatem important (*ibid.*, 362). S. Bonaventure, *loc. cit.*, has a broader formula: quae contra legem Dei sunt.

49. An Anonymous Question, *Vat. lat.* 781 in O. Lottin, *op. cit.*, p. 367; S. Bonaventure, *loc. cit.*

50. Jean de la Rochelle, *Summa de vitiis* (O. Lottin, *op. cit.*, p. 360), gives five categories of acts: acts good in themselves, acts bad in themselves, opera quae sunt bona in genere sed non formata, opera mala in genere sed non deformata, quaedam omnino indifferentia. Conscience obliges in the domain of the last three categories. These ulterior distinctions change nothing of the substance of the theory.

51. Cf. Jean de la Rochelle, *Summa de vitiis* (O. Lottin, *op. cit.*, p. 361); *Toulouse* 737 (*ibid.*, p. 37); *Paris nat. lat.* 14726 (*ibid.*, p. 363).

52. *Summa theologica* quoted by Alexander of Halès (O. Lottin, *op. cit.*, p. 365, note 2); "Non est simile in construendo et destruendo. Quod enim contra conscientiam fit, peccatum est sive demeritum, non tamen omne quod fit secundum conscientiam est bonum et meritorium. Fieri enim secundum conscientiam est, cum creditur esse bonum quod fit; hoc autem non sufficit ad esse bonum: mali enim sumus sufficiens principium, boni autem non sumus sufficiens principium." This is Abelard's position.

53. Jean de la Rochelle, *Summa de vitiis* (O. Lottin, *op. cit.*, p. 360-361).

54. An Anonymous Question, *Vat. lat.* 781 (O. Lottin, *op. cit.*, p. 372).

55. Cf. the edition of the texts in O. Lottin, *op. cit.*, p. 374-385.

56. An Anonymous Question, *Paris nat. lat.* 3804 (text in O. Lottin, *op. cit.*, p. 376).

57. Gauthier de Chateau-Thierry, *Toulouse* 737, in O. Littin, *op. cit.*, p. 380-382 and 383-385.

58. *In II Sent.*, d. 39, q. 3, a. 3.

59. *De Veritate,* q. 17, a. 3, in corp.

60. *Ibid.,* ad 1.

61. *Ibid.,* in corp.

62. Gauthier de Bruges, *Quaestiones disputatae,* q. 12, O. Lottin, *op. cit.,* p. 239 and 399-400. Cf. M. R. Hofmann, *Die Gewissenslehre des Walter von Brügge O.F.M. und die Entwicklung der Gewissenslehre in der Hochscholastik,* Münster, Westf., 1941.

63. *Summa Theol.,* Ia-IIae, q. 19, art. 5 and 6.

64. *Ibid.,* art. 5, to be studied in connection with Ia-IIae, q. 8, art. 1.

65. *Ibid.,* art. 5, ad 2.

66. *Ibid.,* art. 6, to be compared with Ia-IIae, q. 6, art. 8. In this article 6, ad 3, Saint Thomas repeats that the will consequent to an erroneous conscience arising from voluntary ignorance is necessarily bad. However in this case one is not perplexed since one can and must free oneself from the error.

67. *Quaest. quodlib. III,* q. 12, art. 27, in corp. Cf. *De Malo,* q. 3, art. 8.

68. F. Suarez, *Tr. de bon. et mal. hum. act.,* éd. cit., t. IV, p. 445.

69. *Summa Theol.,* Ia-IIae, q. 76, art. 2, *In II Sent.,* d. 22, q. 2, art. 1: "Unicuique peccatum est ignorantia eorum quae ad bonos mores et fidei veritatem pertinent; sed alicui in officio constituto est etiam peccatum ignorantia eorum quae ad suum officium pertinent." *De Malo,* q. 3, art. 7: ea quae fidei sunt ... praecepta decalogi ... quae ad suum officium pertinent.

70. *De Malo,* q. 3, art. 7.

71. Cf. especially: *De Ver.,* q. 17, art. 2; *Quodl. III,* q. 12, art 26 and 27; Ia-IIae, q. 8; q. 19, art. 51 and 6; q. 94, art. 4 and 6; q. 100, art. 1, 3 and 5; *De Malo,* q. 3, art. 8.

72. *De Malo,* q. 3, art. 7.

73. *De Malo,* q. 3, art. 7; Ia-IIae, q. 100, art. 3; art. 5, ad 1.

74. Ia-IIae, q. 100, art. 3, ad 1.

75. *Gal.,* III, 28. Cf. the commentaries on this passage.

76. DB., n. 1292.

77. *De Malo,* q. 3, art. 7. Cfr, *In III Sent.,* d. 25, q. 2, art. 1, sol. 1.

78. L. H. Cornelissen, *Geloof zonder prediking,* Maaseik, 1946, p. 16-109.

79. L. H. Cornelissen, *op. cit.,* p. 47-50.

80. DB., n. 1068.

81. E. Schillebeeckx, *Het niet-begrippelijk moment in de geloofsdaad volgens Thomas van Aquino,* in *Tijdschrift voor Theologie,* t. III, 1963, p. 186.

82. K. Rahner, *Das Christentum und die Nichtchristlichen Religionen,* in *Schriften zur Theologie,* t. V, Einsiedeln, 1962, p. 145-146.

83. J. Maritain, *Raison et raisons*, Paris, 1948, p. 131-165; H. de Lubac, *Sur les chemins de Dieu*, Paris, 1956, p. 120-122.

84. K. Rahner, *op. cit.*, p. 151.

85. *Ibid.*, p. 154.

86. *Ibid.*, p. 156.

THE PERSON IN HIS DIGNITY
AS A MORAL SUBJECT

Man is a dynamic totality and tends toward his proper fulfillment. In the course of his development, the dynamism of his being differentiates into a multitude of particular tendencies. But their multiplicity and their diversity do not condemn him to an incoherent existence, abandoned to the whims of disordered desires. In fact, he is also provided with a moral tendency — the dynamism of the totality as such — which makes him qualified to integrate particular tendencies according to the place and the role which come to them in the development of his personal totality. The capacity of realizing this integration he owes to the fact that he is in the state of having an awareness of the global sense of his existence, of putting *freely* his acts in the service of the fulfillment of this sense and, moreover, of assuming the *responsibility* of the satisfaction or of the sacrifice of his particular tendencies according to the demands of his total destiny. It is precisely this way of being *conscious, free* and *responsible* which confers on him the dignity of *moral subject.*

The qualities which compose our dignity of moral subject are not actuated from the beginning of our existence. Most certainly we can accept, with the psychoanalyst, the presence of an "ideal of myself" from early childhood: unconsciously the child guides himself according to the example of his educators (identification) and he adopts the ideal of life which governs his environment (introjection). But this is not yet a true moral conscience. We can speak all the more of an affective participation in the conception of existence prevailing in the environment or of a "consciousness-mirror" reflecting the ideal of life according to which his parents conducted themselves.

In proportion as one awakens to himself and as one develops his capacity of unprejudiced knowledge and reflection, one will be able to acquire a more and more personal moral conscience. From that time one is obliged to question himself on his personal destiny, on the meaning of his existence. There is a personal question involved: In what does the "ideal of me" consist which I have to realize? The answer which one will attain consititutes a true judgment of conscience. This judgment is not to be confused with the theoretic and scientific thought on the destiny of man in general, such as the philosophy which examines life in the light of reason, and the theology which is concerned with the supernatural destiny of man.[1] All of that can intervene as a norm and as an aid in the formation of the personal judgment of conscience. But this judgment will depend on a large number of strictly individual elements. As a matter of fact the contents of the judgment of conscience on the meaning of personal existence or on the ideal of myself to be realized will be conditioned by the ideal of the non-critical me met with during childhood, by the fact that one has or one has not the faith, by the personal capacity for understanding the requirements of reason and of Revelation, by the turmoil of the passions, by the extent of the repeated efforts that one devotes to the elaboration of an ideal of critical me, by the richness or the absence of personal experience, by the degree of fidelity to the ideal in concrete acts, by the purity of intention, etc. It is clearly, therefore, a true judgment of conscience. It is even the most fundamental judgment of conscience, since, in all the particular acts, it will form the essential criterion of what one has to apprehend in order to remain faithful to the demands of the ideal of me or of what one *believes* to be the meaning of his existence. In other words, we must succeed in shaping a *fundamental judgment of conscience* on the total meaning of our existence in order to be able to develop in detail in its light the *particular judgments of conscience* required in regulating specific acts in conformity with what one considers to be the total meaning of his life, with what in conscience one conceives as the ideal of me to be achieved.

The principal importance of this basic judgment of conscience is made prominent by the indispensable role that it plays in the elaboration of our fundamental choice, that is, our profound choice which we make by ourselves, of the plan of the total end which we are striving for. We are not a simple bundle of multiple and diverse tendencies, but a totality constituting a subject which is one. Hence it follows that spontaneously we aspire to lead an existence as totality, to imprint a specific orientation on our life with the idea of making it a whole in which the multiplicity and diversity of acts serve as elements. Being free, we are able to choose for ourselves the orientation or the meaning that we give to our existence. That is our fundamental choice. This option is a *choice* because it rests with us to determine the inclination of the dominant disposition which will mold the totality of our behavior. This choice must be called *fundamental,* because, all things considered, it is what decides our deeds and our omissions, some particular choices which we will check, and the intention which will support them. A sensual person, his dominant tendency making his desire for enjoyment, will take pleasure only in the acts which bring him immediate delight but will remain insensible on occasions of placing disinterested acts. The miser, enslaved by the desire of possessing, will only really have at heart what is likely to augment his fortune. The one who places himself under the domination of the immoderate desire of making the most of himself (pushing himself forward), will spend his life preoccupied with himself and his glory. In all of these cases, the fundamental choice impresses on life the general direction in which acts and deeds are going to form an integral part. That is why our moral value will depend radically on the moral quality of our fundamental choice. In order to be morally justified this choice will have to consist in making the most of the primacy of the moral tendency, that is, by willing above all moral good for the love of this good.

Now, the elaboration of this moral choice clearly presupposes the formation of what we have called the fundamental judgment of conscience. In fact, it belongs to the very essence of the will (*appetitus rationalis*) to be able to proceed towards the good only insofar as it is known (*bonum apprehensum*). We have observed above with what keenness of understanding St. Thomas — following in this Aristotle — emphasizes that the proper object of the will is not the good such as it is actually in itself (*bonum existens in re*), but the good as known. He concludes from this, still in accordance with Aristotle, that for the will to be borne towards it, it is not required that this always be an actual good, corresponding to the demands of truth, but only that it be understood as such, even if it is not very apparent.[2]

We understand as a consequence the essential importance of the fundamental judgment of conscience: it determines in our actual life the measure of knowledge that we attain concerning moral good, by pursuing, that is, in the total meaning of our existence, the ideal of me to be realized. At all events, if this judgment conditions what we consider ought to be the content of our fundamental choice, our first obligation is to form it sincerely and to perfect it assiduously by trying to scrutinize in a better way the objective requirements of our destiny. Considering, moreover, that it is possible to realize the ideal of moral perfection only in the light of this judgment, we are compelled to follow it faithfully.

What is more, in view of the reciprocity between love and knowledge, the faithfulness with which we pursue what we consider to be the ideal of perfection and the intensity with which we tend to it better are indispensable conditions for better complying with the knowledge of this ideal.

Because of his limitation — a source of ignorance and of eventual errors — the human person is always in search of the truth, without ever possessing it completely. That is why, as Newman said, absolute fidelity to his conscience is the only efficacious way of always assenting still more to the truth.

From all these considerations, it appears that, in order to be faithful to his dignity of *moral subject*, the human person must do his best to form sincerely his fundamental judgment of conscience, and he must follow it faithfully, in order to respond to the obligation that he has of assuming *consciously* and *freely* the *responsibility* of his fundamental choice.

As the fundamental option constitutes a true choice, it is always for us to come back to it, to transform it, to go beyond it. It is in this way that we are capable of freeing ourselves from a previous fundamental choice in order to engage ourselves in a radically transformed option. Being free, we can cause the liberating moment to arise, that marvelous and extraordinary moment, in which the former fundamental choice gives way and in which a completely new plan rises on its ruins. Such a radical modification of the fundamental choice is the total conversion, the one which tranforms us entirely. But there is also the possibility of a perpetual conversion: we are free, in fact, to purify continually our profound choice by maintaining the purity of our intention and the fidelity of our particular acts to the demands of our whole plan.

This leads us to consider more closely the relation between our fundamental choice and the multiplicity of particular acts from which is woven the thread of our existence. In order to understand our particular choices, it is necessary to return to the rule of the fundamental choice which makes of them a characteristic unity synthesis, an organic totality. The causes are numerous which can impede the freedom of our action from exercising itself at the level of the perfection of our profound design. It is the finest example of the distance there can be between the actual and the ideal. But the fact remains that our acts are articulated in a flexible continuity with the profound choice that we made for ourselves: the fundamental choice is truly our *human act* par excellence whose multitude of *particular human* acts are only more or less perfect participations of expressions which, in their way, embody its requirements. Indeed, as long as we shall remain within the framework of a well-fixed fundamental choice, the latter will determine, in the final analysis, the appreciation of the motives which inspire our particular acts and on which precisely we bestow their value from the choice that we have made for ourselves. The particular choices are, therefore, partial structures which do not include each other and which are understood only within the framework of the fundamental choice.

If our particular acts have for an objective to realize, to concretize, to incarnate our fundamental choice, they are able to do it only by being also enlightened, in each new situation, by a judgment of conscience. The will being able to direct itself only on the known good, our particular choices presuppose that in each concrete situation our conscience dictates to us the single act to be placed in order to respond to the demands of what we consider to be the meaning of our total existence, the ideal of me to be realized. Obviously, these judgments of conscience are not infallible. But, even if they are erroneous in good faith, that is to say, if in order to form them we have at heart to seek out the objective truth concerning our acts and if we are animated by the love of moral good, they will be, according to the expression of Suarez, *true from a practical viewpoint* and, then, our successive acts will be morally good and will arise from the virtue that we are striving to practice.[3]

In the area of particular acts, as in that of the fundamental choice, we will therefore be faithful to our dignity of *moral subject* only on the condition of *forming* our judgments of conscience sincerely and of following them faithfully: that is, in fact, the only means of putting *consciously, freely* and in a *responsible* way our particular choices at the service of our fundamental moral choice.

This obligation of following a sincerely formed conscience, even when in good faith it is mistaken, is part of our very being. We have already said that we form a totality, but that our dynamism of the one and indivisible subject is diversified into a multitude of tendencies. The tendencies accordingly constitute some of the structure and partial functions of all that we are. Then, the question arises of knowing how in particular situations our acts can accede to the divergent tendencies without doing harm to our unity. Now, the only way of safeguarding our unity is in all our willing to conform to the judgment of our conscience. Indeed, our intelligence from which our judgment arises, is revealed as a desire of knowing the truth (*appetitus veri*), of disclosing reality such as it is. It is a disinterested faculty, and it submits necessarily to the truth which it grasps or which it thinks it grasps. This is what the scholastics call a necessary faculty.

It is in us like a fixed axis, like an immovable hinge: it is impossible for us to force our intellect to approve our actions when the latter, according to its disinterested judgment, deviate from the truth of moral requirements. Besides, our will is free. Thanks to this freedom we are capable of adapting our acts to the judgment of our intellect, that is to say, conforming them to our conscience: doing this, we respect and safeguard our unity. If, on the contrary, we act against what we consider as the truth, we destroy our unity of subject: in the totality that we are, we bring about a division, a contradiction between our disinterested thought and our free will. We violate therefore our unity of subject. It is precisely the awareness of this internal division which constitutes the essence of remorse. Abelard was not wrong in asserting that the rupture or the contradiction between the conviction of conscience, which recognizes what is to be done, and the consent knowingly and freely given to what we think of as forbidden, belongs to the very essence of the sin.

On the whole we can conclude that, in his dignity of moral subject, the human person is always responsible for his effective love of the moral good.

1. Considering that he is able to will this good only in the measure in which he knows it, he has the obligation of taking seriously the formation of the judgments of conscience — an essential condition for submitting his acts to the requirements of the moral good.

2. As he tries sincerely to form his judgment of conscience and to conform his will faithfully to it, his act is under any circumstances a fruit of his love for moral good and, consequently, good and virtuous, even if in good faith it flows from a judgment of an erroneous conscience, his condition as *human* subject being limited and therefore fallible.

3. Being a totality, he is *responsible* for the conformity of his *free* activity with the judgment of *conscience*, an essential requirement of his dignity as *moral* subject.

These considerations bring out the most essential moral requirement of all the relationships between human persons: *each one must be esteemed and treated as a moral subject.*

This obligation entails first of all that we must respect

every man as an *autonomous* subject. Assuredly the person is not autonomous in this sense that his conscience would constitute his supreme norm. We have ceased to insist, on the contrary, on the obligation of forming his conscience sincerely in order to make his judgments coincide more and more perfectly with the objective requirements of the moral norm. But man is autonomous in the sense that he is personally *responsible* for the conformity of his *free* acts with the judgment of *conscience*. Thanks to this autonomy he disposes and decides for himself concerning its moral value. In other words, his moral perfection can be promoted or violated only in accordance with the judgment put forward by his own conscience on the moral quality of that which he himself does. What takes place in his behavior, without the intervention of his conscience, of his liberty, and, consequently, of his responsibility, is not even an *actus humanus*, but a simple *actus hominis*, breaking away from his autonomy and not affecting his moral destiny.

In order to be accepted in conformity with his intrinsic dignity, every human person must therefore be treated as an autonomous subject. This principle proves so universally true, that it still always calls for the attitude to be taken with respect to those who have not yet attained the exercise of their autonomy. Is it not true that education is an aid for the purpose of promoting the attainment of personal autonomy? Respect for the vocation of each man to personal autonomy is the most important requirement of all interpersonal relations.

An autonomous subject, the person is also *irreplaceable*. It is the person himself who assumes the responsibility for the realization or for the failure of his moral development, according as he conforms or opposes his free behavior to the judgment of his conscience. Because of the immanence of his conscious and free acts, which determine precisely his moral worth, he is irreplaceable. Of course he can receive the help of others on his way towards truth and in the formation of his will. However, this help will be truly beneficial to him only on condition that he succeeds in accepting and assimilating it into his conscious and free attitudes. If, therefore, one takes someone's place in order to replace him owing to initiative of which he is not yet capable, or to protect him against himself — we will say that the exercise of authority involves this subsitutional role — we will bring him a true pedagogical help when we will have led him to improve his own capacity of acting from his own immanence.

As a moral subject, the person is finally *inviolable*. Today, techniques are not lacking which permit the violation of the integrity of the subjective inner nature. Under the influence of hypnosis, and, still more, by the administration of barbiturates, we can put someone in a twilight state in which he is not capable of acting as a moral subject, but only of reacting automatically to questions asked or to orders given. Even in such a situation in which we take away from him the possibility of acting consciously, freely and in a responsible way, the human person preserves his intangibility in this sense that the acts which the sole constraint extorts from him are powerless to injure his moral perfection. What can violate these techniques is the human quality of the impersonal relations worthy of a moral subject. Indeed, man is called to assume the responsibility of his social relations, by himself determining consciously and freely his attitudes, his words and his acts with respect to others. Social relations lose their specifically human character, as soon as they no longer fulfill the conditions of an encounter of conscious and free subjects. Let us give an example. The relations of the witnesses and of the accused with the judge, being relations of human persons, are made of attitudes and of conscious and free conduct for which each one of them has to assume respectively personal responsibility. If therefore in order to facilitate the interrogation or to extort the confession, one places the witnesses or the accused in a hypnotic state, one violates their dignity as a moral subject by imposing upon them social relations which are no longer at the level of the relations suitable to human persons. What is more, the witnesses and the accused have not even the right to lend themselves to such a practice, their dignity as moral Subjects forbidding them to renounce, in their relations with others, the human prerogatives which are awareness, freedom and responsibility. Such intervention can be justified only in the case in which it promotes or protects in the person himself the possibility of bearing oneself as a moral subject. It is in this way that the use of technical means will be lawful, either when it is indicated in a surgical operation assuring the bodily health or life of the *subject*, or to anaesthetize pain, or finally as helping in a psychotherapeutic treatment for reestablishing the psychological equilibrium of the *moral* subject. In other cases, relative not to the internal good but to the behavior of the person in his relationships, it would constitute a violation of the conscious inner character, lowering the moral subject to the level of an object, the person to that of an automaton.

These basic principles establish the very foundation of personal rights and the order according to which the persons are to be placed in relation to each other.

Each one must realize the meaning of his existence (the ideal of me). Therein lies his personal destiny.

From the *subjective* point of view this destiny is personal because each one must realize it *personally*, namely, in his quality as a moral, conscious, free and responsible moral subject; and, consequently, in the eyes of others, autonomous, irreplaceable, and inviolable. Since each one must achieve his destiny personally, the relations between human persons will be ordered only on the condition of resting on the recognition of the dignity as moral subjects of all those who are included in it. It is therefore the *duty* of each one to respect and treat the other as a moral subject, just as it is, correlatively, the right of each one to be treated by others as a moral subject. It is due to his condition and his dignity as a moral subject that each person is subject by right.

From the objective point of view, the destiny of each man is personal, since it consists in the realization of the perfection of the person as such, of what, according to rational and revealed truth, is suitable to the person considered in his relationships in the world, to others, to social groups, to God, and in himself as incarnate spirit. By elaborating the meaning of all these aspects of his being, the person realizes his moral perfection. The demands of this perfection form the object of his personal duty and, in the presence of others, they determine the content of his personal *rights*.

We cannot speak of personal rights as long as they disregard relationships with others. Our condition of moral subject and the requirements of our destiny are, for ourselves, a source of duty and of obligation. They are expressed in terms of duty only from the moment in which, in our social relationships, they assert themselves in the presence of others. The right is therefore a social category. It is used here only in a social context, namely, in our relations with others or with a social group. In other words, our rights have value only in the measure in which other persons or groups have duties of justice in our regard. We have expressed the essential content of these duties by saying that each one must be respected and treated by others as a moral subject. But how far does this obligation of others extend in our regard? The question is all the more important and delicate because we are able to conduct ourselves as moral subjects only by following the judgment of our sincerely formed conscience. Now, this judgment can be erroneous in good faith. No doubt even in this case we can say, in deference to Suarez, that it is true from a practical viewpoint and consequently right, and that the consequent act is good and virtuous. But it is no less true that going back to another expression of Suarez, this act is materially bad. In spite of its subjective goodness, such an act causes an objective disorder, susceptible of harm to others and of injuring the interests of the groups to which we belong. When, for example, a writer is convinced of the absolute independence of artistic values with regard to the moral and literary value of his pornographic writings and he publishes and circulates them, his action will have a pernicious reaction on a large number of readers. Of course the negative effect would not be very considerable, if everyone were sufficiently formed to appraise his reading in an autonomous manner. But in every community we will always have some young people and some simple people incapable of a critical attitude. Must they be protected by those who have the responsibility of the good of the group? Can this protection go as far as limiting the freedom of action of this writer who is convinced of his legitimate right? In what measure and according to what criterion can restrictions be imposed?

In order to answer these questions, we must envisage the person as a social being for the purpose of examining how the social exigencies affect his condition as a moral subject.

---

1. In the *Summa Theologica*, Ia-IIae, Saint Thomas puts in first place his *Tractatus de ultimo fine seu de beatitudine* (q. 1-5), in order to have in the following place the *Tractatus de humanis actibus* (q. 6-21). This order is perfectly justified. It is necessary, in fact, to examine first of all the *global sense of human existence* in order to throw light on the *fundamental judgment of conscience* relative to the human act par excellence which is the *fundamental choice*. Then, in the light of the requirements of the total or ultimate end of existence, one can look for the moral norms which preside over particular human acts and which

must govern the formation of the *particular judgments of conscience* by means of which the fundamental choice will be expressed and embodied in many particular acts.

2. *Summa Theol.*, Ia-IIae, q. 8, art. 1. Cf. *supra*, p. 34

3. Cf. what we have said concerning the *recta conscientia* according to Suarez, *supra*. pp. 11-16 and 38.

CHAPTER 4

THE PERSON AS A
SOCIAL BEING

The influence of individualism still acts deceitfully, when one considers man from one point of view, society from another, and when after doing this, one tries to establish the relationship between the two. According to this conception, the human person is perfected and fulfilled in himself only by maintaining purely extrinsic relations with society.

To follow this path is to create a false problem. Indeed, man is not exterior to his relations. He is an essentially open reality. He has experience of himself only by having experience with others. We say, nowadays, that he is conscious of himself only by being intentionally conscious. Even if it wishes to look at itself, the conscience is not able to take stock of itself without itself referring to an object: it is present to itself by being present to something else.[1]

In order to understand the import of this truth in the domain of our social relations it suffices to recall a few basic ideas of genetic psychology, showing that it is only in and by intentional awareness that consciousness of self awakens. From the beginning of his life the child is open to his surroundings and he already participates in what happens around him before taking possession of himself. On account of his need for tenderness, protection and security, he is in affective symbiosis with his surroundings. The psychologists verify from the delays and from the deviations in his development when he feels the frustration of his need for affection. Soon this affective intentionality is sustained, strengthened and broadened, thanks to the contact that seeing and hearing (perceptive intentionality) furnish it: in the intimate relationship which he carries on with his mother, the child feels his disposition deeply affected on her account in his mimicry, his expression, his gestures, the tone of his voice.

All the human and therefore cultural realities which surround him and in which he participates by his affectivity are a continuous appeal to the awakening of the awareness of himself. Actually, from his second year the child succeeds more and more in understanding the meaning of the words which are addressed to him, the intended purpose of the objects which he sees handled around him, the meaning of the actions placed in his surroundings. Now, to understand is to tell *himself* what things mean, what distinguishes *himself* from known reality, to assent to the awareness of himself. We could say that the child is able to attain a conscious existence only by contact with those who have already reached a conscious life. Suffice it to refer to the infrahuman stage of the "wild children," snatched and brought up by wild beasts.[2] In his intentional consciousness, affective and perceptive, the child has to be exposed to a human environment to succeed in taking possession of himself. That is so true that we meet with particular difficulties in awakening to conscious life the children deprived of the most important possibilities of perceptive awareness. This is the case of children who are blind and deaf from birth. Formerly, we called them "imprisoned souls," because we considered them incapable of conscious life. Today, we know that they are perfectly normal, but that special methods must be used in order to lead them to the awakening of their consciousness. Making use above all of the sense of touch to open intentionally the doors to reality, it is principally by pressing on their hands with certain gestures and in certain positions that we succeed in having them *understand* signs and therefore awaken their awareness of themselves.[3] We can therefore conclude that, from birth, man is an essentially social being. Seeing that he begins in this world by living in affective union with his social surroundings, he is already social before discovering himself. What is more, it is only under the stimulation of his authentic relations with a human environment that he is able to wake up to conscious and personal existence.

In the past certain psychologists held that autism was the orignal disposition of the child: in the beginning he would be completely shut up within himself and he would become social only in the course of his development. Present-day knowledge has completely abandoned this conception.[4] The child does not have to be socialized; he is social from the first moments of his life. It is only from his affective symbiosis with a human environment that he will be raised progressively to the level of consciousness of self. From this moment he will become more and more capable of taking a conscious and free attitude with respect to his social ties. Surely, it is not a question of absolute freedom. Although one is a social being from the beginning of his life, although one has been formed in the structure of a determined milieu, although one is already the product of existing ties, these are imposed as a necessity. But the consent to this necessity is already a free attitude. However, the influence of freedom extends much further than the simple acceptation of what is given in actual fact. Indeed, the awakening of our consciousness of ourselves constitutes our promotion to the condition and to the dignity of moral subject. Being conscious, free and consequently responsible we are no longer simply parts of a social whole. That was our situation as long as we were incapable of distinguishing ourselves from our environment. We are called to *take* part in the social life. Our social nature is no longer a simple fact, it becomes a duty and a vocation directing an appeal to our freedom. In other words, having the prerogatives of moral subjects, we can and must search in conscience for the meaning of our social relations and assume the responsibility of free acts required for accepting and fostering the fulfillment of this meaning.

Our existence is therefore basically social from its beginning. During our early childhood our social environment was at that point indispensable because it belonged to our environment to awaken our awareness of ourselves. Once this awareness develops, the social links remain no less essential. But a radical change is produced: henceforth they engage our personal responsibility. It is in our quality as moral subjects that we have to assume the elaboration of our social relations. We will accomplish this mission by satisfying the demands of the "common good" of the groups to which we belong.

The examination of our social nature further complicates the question which we have already asked. If each person must be respected and treated by others and by groups as a moral subject, how far does this obligation extend? To what extent can we come to a conclusion concerning the freedom of those who, while following in good faith an erroneous conscience, posit nevertheless acts contrary to the meaning of their social relations? How can we gain from the human person the accomplishment of obligations arising from his social nature without bringing harm to his dignity as a moral subject? These questions bring us to the very heart of the problem of freedom of conscience.

---

1. Fr. J. Brecht, *Bewusstsein und Existenz. Wesen und Weg der Phänomenologie*, Bremen, 1948, p. 26, stresses that F. Brentano, who reintroduced the idea of *intentionality* into present-day philosophy, made a study on philosophy in the Middle Ages. Just as Descartes drew his attention to the importance of the conscience, likewise the scholastic

tradition showed him how intentionality is an essential property of this conscience. Let us note especially two texts of Saint Thomas. *In I Sent.*, d. 1, q. 2, a. 1, ad 2: "Eadem operatione intelligo intelligibile et intelligo me intelligere." *De Ver.*, q. 10, a. 8: "Nullus autem percipit se intelligere nisi ex hoc quod aliquid intelligit: quia prius est intelligere aliquid quam intelligere se intelligere."

2. A. Demaison, *Le livre des enfants sauvages*, Paris, 1953. Cf. especially the very interesting study of A. Gesell, *Wolf Child and Human Child*, London, 1942.

3. M. Blondel, *La Pensée*, Paris, 1948, t. I, p. 69-95 and 333-338; A. Marc, *Psychologie réflexive*, Paris, 1949, t. I, pp. 19-32

4. Concerning this subject, read the beautiful pages of A. Kriekemans, *Principes de l'éducation religieuse, sociale, et morale*, Louvain, 1955, p. 124-166.

CHAPTER 5

FREEDOM OF CONSCIENCE

From all that we have already said it appears that three important elements dominate the crucial question of freedom of conscience.

First of all, being limited and being subject to the consequences of original sin, the human person is exposed to ignorance and to error. He can be deceived in good faith, even in his judgment of conscience concerning the most essential decisions of his existence.

Moreover, in order to be faithful to his dignity as a moral subject, he has the obligation of sincerely forming his judgment of conscience and of following it faithfully, even if in good faith he is mistaken, since it is only on this condition that he can realize his personal destiny. This obligation is the source of freedom of conscience, which therefore consists in placing free actions in conformity with the judgment of conscience, but which would be merely illusory if the social environment did not guarantee it.

Nevertheless, being a social being, the person must assume and promote the objective sense of his social relations. That is also part of his personal destiny. Perhaps, while being perfectly consistent with himself, he places actions which are materially evil, bringing harm to others or disturbing the social order. In this case, what he does as a *moral subject* is opposed to the objective requirements of what he has to accomplish as a *social being*. How can we resolve this contradiction?

The contradiction is all the more difficult to overcome since it arises from two aspects of the same personal destiny. Considered from the subjective point of view this destiny requires that the person be faithful to his conscience and respect his dignity as a moral subject. Looked at from the objective point of view this same destiny requires the realization of the objective sense of social relations, because the person is a social being and the accomplishment of the meaning of his social relationships composes an integral part of his moral perfection, that is, of the demands of the norm of morality.

The conflict can be reduced immediately as long as the resources of education prove effective. We said that the person as a moral subject is autonomous, irreplaceable and inviolable. Far from violating the autonomy of the person, the purpose of education is to render him capable of directing himself. Up-bringing requires a substitutional function — during the first period of life, for example, the parents have to take the place of the child and think and act in his place — but this function is temporary and tends to become superfluous. If it becomes permanent, it would be necessary to conclude that the training failed in its very objective, which consists in leading to maturity and to autonomy. However, as no one is able to attain a perfect competence and autonomy in all spheres of human activity, we need pedagogical help during our whole existence. That is why the exercise of authority includes an educational function. This role consists in helping the inexperienced to understand the requirements of their social relations and to desire their fulfillment in such a way that what they consider their duty as moral subjects coincides more and more with their actual obligations as social beings.

But what is to be done if the educative help remains ineffectual? What must be the attitude of authority when, in spite of everything, certain members of society consider themselves obliged in conscience to place acts which are contrary to the true demands of their social relations? How far can lawful restraint be extended?

By way of introduction to the answer to this question, it is not without interest to recall the conception of St. Thomas on the subject of human laws. No doubt, he did not state the problem which interests us here. But the examination of the restrictions which, *in the name of morality*, are imposed on the powers of the legislator, will furnish us with some invaluable information.

No doubt that for St. Thomas the domain of human laws arises from the moral order. The juridical order, determined by positive law, constitutes an integral part of morality, namely, the area of justice which regulates objective relations according to the demands of morality: "Hoc medium rei est etiam medium rationis et ideo in iustitia salvatur ratio virtutis moralis." [1] Moreover, St. Thomas defines positive law as "quaedam ordinatio rationis ad bonum commune ab eo qui curam communitatis habet promulgata." [2] Law acts by reason and prescribes the order of reason, which is the very definition of morality. But it does not reproduce all the moral prescriptions; it is concerned with the moral order from the formally social point of view. In other words, it asserts the moral demands concerning the protection and promotion of the common good. [3]

If the juridical order comes from the moral order, it follows that the restrictions which by chance will be imposed on the powers of the law, will be limited also by the requirements of morality. In a general way St. Thomas affirms that it is morality which requires that human law not mix with what it is incapable of ruling. [4] To be convinced of the importance which he attaches to this principle, it suffices to consider the various applications which he makes of it.

Considering that the juridical order is an integral part of the moral order, it is evidently necessary to emphasize beforehand that a human law would be necessarily bad if it approved what morality forbids, *si approbaret ea quae lex aeterna reprobat*.[5]

But this reservation does not mean that human law should not tolerate and leave unpunished a good many morally unlawful actions. If, on the one hand, it is never able to approve what moral law forbids, on the other hand, neither can it defend all that morality rejects: *"Lex humana non omnia potest prohibere quae prohibet lex naturae."* [6]

St. Thomas explicitly considers whether it is within the competence of human law to curb all vices.[7] In order to justify his negative answer he merely calls upon some principles of the moral order.

First of all, the legislator would commit a reprehensible act by promulgating a law whose observance would be impossible: *"Lex debet esse possibilis."* Law is intended for the totality of the population, a large part of which is far from being perfect in virtue. That is why it does not prohibit all the vices which virtuous people avoid, but only the most serious which we can discourage for most people. It principally bans acts injurious to others and what must be forbidden in order to safeguard the human community, such as murder and stealing;[8] it leaves unpunished some other offenses, such as fornication.[9]

One impairs the love of moral good when one places acts causing more harm than good. In this connection St. Thomas, citing the authority of St. Augustine, declares that human law can neither prohibit nor punish all evil actions. In fact, by trying to root out all evil, it would also hinder the furtherance of the common good.[10] Is it not true that the majority of the imperfect fall into more serious depravity if intolerable restrictions are imposed? The only effect would be contempt of the law, and contempt is a source of the greatest evils.[11]

St. Thomas often repeats that the intention of the legislator has a bearing above all and principally on the common good,[12] that is, on the requirements of social life which are security,[13] the obligation of giving to each individual his due and of refraining from injustices,[14] harmony and friendship among the members of society,[15] tranquility and peace in the community.[16] But, following Aristotle, he adds that by proposing to himself this objective, the legislator pursues and achieves at the same time a pedagogical end. Clearly the law prescribes directly the practice of virtues only insofar as it insists on external acts required with an eye to the common good. But, through these acts, the legislator has another purpose; he is aiming for the attainment of virtue in those under his jurisdiction.[17] The law, by imposing discipline and punishing transgressions, induces the habit of performing virtuous actions. The pedagogical value of the habit consists in this, that what was at first carried out through fear of punishment is not practiced of one's own free will. The subject finds joy in these virtuous acts and becomes in that way more virtuous.[18] However, in order to bring about this result, the legislator has to respect the pedagogical law of gradation: "Lex humana intendit homines inducere ad virtutem, non subito, sed gradatim." [19] In other words, the legislator will not be able to discourage the majority of citizens; he will have to take into account the moral level which is attainable by them; he will begin by prohibiting the actions most harmful to the common good and progressively he will try to turn those under his jurisdiction away from evil in order that they may succeed in practicing virtue of their own free will, *ut gradatim homines retracti a malis per seipsos ad virtutem exerceantur.*[20]

It has been written that "contrary to morality, the law is obliged often to sacrifice respectable things — sometimes even including justice — to the clearly social necessity of the maintenance of a certain exterior order which is the condition for all the rest." There may be a necessity beforehand, for "some very serious reasons in order that the positive law, in the regulating of private interests, ignore the moral law of justice" and "if it is done, it will have to make efforts to reduce to a strict minimum the exceptions recognized as indispensable." [21] The meaning of such assertions remains equivocal, as long as we do not add that the indispensable exceptions are precisely imposed by the demands of the moral order. It is in the name of morality that it is necessary to ask the legislator not to let himself be attracted by an illusory perfectionism, to recognize the relativity of human laws and to impose restrictions on their application, even concerning the prohibition of objective evil.

How far, then, can legal restraints be extended in regard to actions materially evil as a natural consequence of a judgment of conscience erroneous in good faith? What are the requirements and the limits of freedom of conscience? It seems to us that from the point of view of morals, all the elements of the answer are grouped under three headings.

I — AS MUCH FREEDOM AS POSSIBLE

Following our considerations on the human person, envisaged in his condition and in his dignity as moral subject, we must take as a point of departure the recognition of freedom of conscience. To express this principle in a concrete fashion, it is necessary to allow as a basis of social life the widest possible development of the free initiative of persons as much in their individual activities as in those of the groups to which they freely adhere.

In order to back up this thesis, let us gather together the reasons developed in the course of our account. Raised to the dignity of a moral subject, the human person is able to pursue his moral perfection only by assuming the responsibility of conforming his free acts to the judgment of his conscience. He still enriches this moral perfection even if, in spite of the care which he devotes to the search for truth, he forms and follows an erroneous conscience. In this case he still actually desires moral good and he perfects himself by acting out of love for this good. Even then, he develops his fidelity to truth, because he is able to put his acts in the service of truth only insofar as the latter penetrates them and directs them through the judgment of his conscience. Being limited and fallible, the person is not necessarily responsible for his error concerning the demands of moral good; however, he is always responsible for the love that he bears to truth and to the good, and every act which embodies this love increases his moral perfection. Theoretically, we must therefore allow that the person is acting in conformity with his judgment of conscience, even if the latter is erroneous and in good faith, because, even then, it is the love of moral good which animates what he does, and it is precisely the maintainance of this love which promotes his moral perfection.[22]

Proclaiming freedom of conscience as a fundamental principle, we are not advocating moral indifferentism. On the contrary, we are emphasizing that it is only the love of moral good which can constitute the perfection of the person. But the person will put this love into practice only in his condition as moral subject, and the respect and the esteem which we require for the moral subject is anything but indifferentism. Let no one object either that the recognition of freedom of conscience leads necessarily to individualism. We have not ceased to stress that the destiny of the person consists in developing as open reality: it is only by elaborating the objective meaning of all his relations that he fulfills himself. But, once again, all this affects his moral perfection only insofar as he is involved in it as a moral subject. Freedom of conscience is only the guarantee and the protection of the dignity of the moral subject in his social relations.

However, this proclamation of freedom of conscience is only a point of departure. It states the first principle to which we shall have recourse; it leaves its application to be delicately expressed by other objectively valid requirements. That is why we say: *as much freedom as possible.* In fact the measure of freedom will have to be determined by taking into account all of the values which must be protected. Some reservations will be imposed in virtue of the demands of the common good, which we shall speak of later.

II — FREEDOM IN OBLIGATION

When the legislator exercises his power in applying restrictions on the freedom of action of those under his jurisdiction, the obligations imposed must never go beyond what is necessary and must leave as wide a margin as possible for freedom. This is but a special application of the principle: as much freedom as possible.

An example will illustrate this assertion. It is evident that the formation of young people is of capital importance in order that a society may safeguard and raise its cultural level. Therefore, authority has the right to introduce the obligation of school attendance up to a definite age according as economic conditions allow for it. By doing this authority exercises a substitutional function: it substitutes itself for the parents, on whom rests the duty and the right of educating their children;

it makes a decision and uses, as far as is necessary, the restraints needed to have the decision respected. Such intervention is legitimate. In fact, in a question of such great social importance, authority protects the parents against their own negligence. But it would go too far if it did not leave to the latter the freedom of founding or of choosing the schools which, with respect to convictions, gives the guarantee of rightly prolonging the family education. Freedom in obligation is therefore necessary and as much freedom as possible.

III — THE NEEDS OF THE COMMON GOOD

The common good is constituted by the *complex of the requirements of life in society*. But what is life in society? First of all, it implies necessarily a *coexistence* of persons and their groupings, it is a "life together." It includes also a cooperation, a *collaboration* in the realization of cultural values. It involves finally a *coparticipation* in which the members have a share in the fruits of the collaboration. The common good is therefore the totality of the demands of coexistence, of collaboration and of coparticipation. It is the proper mission of authority to promote the common good. That is why it is qualified to impose on persons and their groupings all that is appropriate to the realization of the common good, all that is truly necessary or useful for coexistence, collaboration and coparticipation. But in the accomplishment of this task it will treat its subordinates in conformity with their dignity as moral subjects by relying as much as possible on the conscious and free initiative for which they assume personal responsibility. As a result it will guarantee as much as possible the exercise of freedom of conscience and will use only restrictions necessary for providing that the moral subjects behave as *social beings*.

A. The Requirements of Coexistence

Life in society is first of all the coexistence of persons and of groupings of persons. This coexistence presents a wide variety of forms and modalities, which are the object of sociology and of social psychology. The intimate coexistence in the bosom of the family reveals a much greater intensity than that of a group of workers who are together merely during the hours of work or that of citizens of a country who, while having perhaps no direct connection between themselves, coexist in the same political regime. What interests us especially here is the fact that the coexistence of men assumes a broader extension in proportion as culture progresses. In our days an actual coexistence embraces the whole of humanity. The perfection of the means of transportation does away with distances. The means of communication, such as the telephone, telegraph, press, radio, television, can make us more "present" at events taking place on other continents than at the work of our neighbor in the house next door. The cultural exchanges between regions and people is increasing and extending. Since we have in our possession arms whose use would mean collective suicide, we feel more and more that "peaceful coexistence" on a worldwide level is a question of life or death. Consequently, it is not astonishing that all nations are beginning to realize that coexistence, on a worldwide scale, requires a moral basis and a juridical superstructure.

In what does the moral basis of all human coexistence consist? One of the most marvelous manifestations of our coexistence is the dialogue. The simple fact of being able to talk with others and to understand each other has a profound signification.

As soon as we engage in conversation with someone, it is because we are both interested in the same object or give importance to the same matter. On that subject we exchange our ideas, our feelings, our desires, our free opinions. Conversation shows us in this way that the other person is very much like us, an *alter ego*, who also thinks, feels, is free and responsible, receptive to values, capable of probing within himself for the meaning of his existence in the world with others, etc.

Conversation shows us that we meet each other on the same level, as equals or, according to an expression in vogue today, we share the same human condition. In other words, our coexistence or our being-with-others shows to our unbiased thinking a fundamental meaning: the other person is not a means, as are objects in the world; he is a subject, a person, a counterpart, a neighbor.

But the dialogue does not show only our basic equality; it also places in a prominent position the originality of each individual. It becomes obvious when the conversation unfolds under the form of a discussion. This discussion must involve a point of contact with regard to the same object, under pain of dissolving into a futile quarrel of words from the moment that we are no longer talking about the same thing. The fact that we are able to meet regarding the same topic of conversation presupposes our fundamental equality. But this fact does not exhaust all the richness contained in the possibility of the discussion. The latter implies, moreover, that we are not entirely in agreement, that, with regard to the same subject, our conceptions, our feelings, our attitudes and our reactions differ. Although basically alike, we are therefore also different. Each person is an original being, an individual and irreplaceable subjectivity. Nowadays psychology is concerned with studying more closely the sources of this originality. It stresses that each man has his constitution, his temperament, his capacities, his tendencies, and that, in proportion as he assumes and develops his orignal talents, he develops into a unique personality having a character of his own.

This simple analysis of the universal phenomenon known as conversation reveals to us the fundamental meaning of our existence. It is obvious that we are untrue to this meaning if we exploit others as an object or as a means of our own profit or pleasure. Respect for this meaning requires that we treat each person as a subject who is at the same time both an equal and an original personality.

It is by putting love into practice that we acknowledge and develop the complete meaning of our relations with others.

Without doubt, love offers a rich diversity of forms and modalities. The nuances are numerous and varied, especially from the affective point of view, in conjugal love, between fiances, love between parents and children, love between friends, love of neighbor, etc. But in every case certain essential conditions are fulfilled in order that it may be possible to speak of love.

In the first place, an element essential in all love is the attitude, the disposition which we have in order to esteem and value the other as a person. It is what, nowadays, we call the recognition of man by man. All love is based on a deep respect which makes us appreciate the other person at the same time both as our equal in human dignity and as an original personality, and which prevents us from lowering him to the level of an object or of a means.

In the second place, it belongs to the essence of all love to desire advancement. St. Thomas writes that loving someone is to wish him well. Certainly the end of our love is the person loved himself; but if the love is real, it desires that the person attain the perfection of which he is capable — *amor quo amatur aliquid ut ei sit bonum* — or, if it is aimed at God, it takes pleasure in his perfection and rejoices in his fullness.

These elements of a philiosophy of love are perfected by the doctrines of Christian revelation.

Let us take note first of all that Christ refers to the requirements of love on the human level when He proclaims the precept: "Love your neighbor as yourself" (Matt. 22:39). He made the content of this precept clearer himself by stating what Christians have the habit of calling the "golden rule" of charity: "Therefore, all that you wish me to do to you, even so do you also to them" (Matt. 7:12). The Master knows that we are very sensitive to all that concerns ourselves and the attitude of others toward us. He asks us to manifest the same sensitivity concerning the good of others. Thus Christ brings out the human aspect of love. Also, is it not astonishing that we meet again in substance this "golden rule" among a large number of non-Christian people [23] and that the scholastics had considered it as a first principle of natural law?

But Christian revelation is not limited to throwing light on the human demands of love of our neighbor. Our Lord has also expressed the theological dimensions: "A new commandment I give you: that as I have loved you, you also love one another" (John 23:34). Fraternal charity forms the object of a new precept, appropriate to Christ, insofar as it is the imitation of the love of Christ. Now this love is the manifestation of the charity which the Father has for us. It is consequently from this charity that the Christian will have to discern the quality of love of neighbor.

Concerning the charity of the Father, St. John writes: "God is love. In this has the love of God been shown in our case, that God has sent His only-begotten Son into the world that we may live through Him. In this is the love, not that we have loved God, but that He has first loved us, and sent His Son a propitiation for our sins" (I John 4:8-10). St. Paul defines the love of the Father in the same way: "But God commends His charity towards us, because when as yet we were sinners, Christ died for us" (Rom. 5:8-10). Such is the love of the Father. It gives, and the gift consists in the Father sending us His own Son for our salvation. It pardons and reconciles, and for that purpose it becomes a love-offering as Christ is sacrificed for our sins. Being sinners and as such enemies of God, we in no way merit this love which is, therefore, a free gift, a pardon, a grace, an unselfish and generous gift of the Father.

We share in this love of the Father because "the charity of God is poured forth in our hearts by the Holy Spirit Who has been given to us" (Rom. 5:5). When St. Paul speaks of the fruits of the Holy Spirit in us he names charity first (Gal. 5:22), and he will say that it is incomparably superior to every charism of the Holy Spirit (I Cor. 13:1-11).

Partaking of the charity of the Father, our love will be, by that very fact, an imitation of it. If our charity toward our neighbor has its source in God —"for love is from God, and everyone who loves is born of God" (I John 4:7) — it will also show the qualities of the love of the Father. It will be a gift, a pardon, a reconciliation. It will also be free and generous, as the love of the Father was when we were still sinners and enemies. If someone has the Spirit within him, his acts of love will emanate from two sources: they are from God because they have their origin in participation in the charity of the Father; they are also his own acts as he is using his freedom to spread around himself the love of the Father in which he is participating. Each act of Christian charity is in some way the sacrament, the sacred and effective sign by whose mediation the love of the Father reaches men. If we live the meaning of our Christian existence, we will conduct ourselves in such a way as to radiate the love of the Father in which we are *sharing* and which we are *imitating*.

Let us now speak of the fundamental texts of the New Testament concerning love of our fellowmen. "But I say to you, love your enemies, do good to those who hate you, and pray for those who persecute and culumniate you, so that you may be children of your Father in heaven, Who makes His sun to rise on the good and evil and sends rain on the just and the unjust. . . . You therefore are to be perfect, even as your heavenly Father is perfect" (Matt. 5:43-48). If our charity is a participation in that of the Father, we understand that we must resemble the Father as His children and imitate the perfection of His love.

"Therefore, if thou art offering thy gift at the altar and there thou rememberest that thy brother has anything against thee, leave thy gift before the altar and go first to be reconciled to thy brother, and then come and offer thy gift" (Matt. 5:23-24). If my brother has something against me, according to purely human standards, it is up to him to take the initiative for a reconciliation. Christian charity demands that I, in spite of every difficulty, make the first move in order that my prayer and my sacrifice may be agreeable to God. One day St. Peter asked a question concerning specifically the matter of pardon: "Lord, if my brother sins against me, how many times will I pardon him. To justify this demand, He told a parable. A king has just canceled payment of a considerable debt owed by an insolvent servant. Immediately afterwards the servant reveals himself as being without pity toward a fellow-servant who owes him a small sum. The king hears of it, calls him, and treats him with ruthless severity. And Jesus concludes: "So also my heavenly Father will do to you, if you do not each forgive your brothers from your hearts" (Matt. 18:21-35). We ask the Father in vain to forgive us our sins if we do not forgive our fellow men.

St. Paul gives us a magnificent synthesis of the requirements of Christian charity: "Do not grieve the Holy Spirit of God in whom you were sealed for the day of redemption. Let all bitterness, and wrath, and indignation, and clamor, and reviling be removed from you, along with all malice." A Christian cannot commit sins against fraternal charity which are opposed to the Holy Spirit through Whom the love of the Father has been sown in our heart. After condemning these negative attitudes, the Apostle describes the positive disposition of Christian charity and its divine motivation: "Be kind to one another and merciful, generously forgiving one another as also God in Christ has generously forgiven you. Be you, therefore, imitators of God, as very dear children. Walk in love, as Christ also loved us and delivered himself up for us an offering and a sacrifice to God to ascend in fragrant odor" (Ephes. 4:30, 5:1-2).

Just as Christ mentions the human aspect of love by demanding love of our neighbor as ourself, so St. Paul similarly acknowledges the importance of the human qualities of love, and by the examples which he gives he sees the second tablet of the law, that is, the whole set of commandments concerning human coexistence, summed up in these words: "Thou shalt love thy neighbor as thyself" (Rom. 13:8-10). The human qualities of love must be integrated into Christian charity, which must take on the demands of a truly human coexistence: charity is patient, kind, humble, not ambitious, is concerned with justice and truth, bears with all things, endures all things (I Cor. 13:4-7).

If love is the essential foundation of all human coexistence, it is love which, in our relations with others, must determine our attitude in regard to freedom of conscience.

First of all, love includes the tendency which makes us appreciate and value others in the light of their dignity as human persons. Now, this dignity consists fundamentally in the fact that each person is a *moral subject*, called to assume the responsibility for the conformity of his free acts to the judgment of his conscience. Love requires, therefore, respect for every person in his dignity as a moral subject. Assuredly, persuaded of the truth of our Christian conviction, we are in no way able to sanction the other conceptions of life and of the world insofar as they clash at the same time with Christian revelation. Love rejoices in truth and feels a loathing for error.

But what we can and must respect and esteem in those who do not share our conviction is that they are acting as *moral subjects* by faithfully following their conscience which they are striving to form sincerely. If this attitude of respect is already necessary on the level of purely human love, it must be evident for those who are convinced that they are sharing in the love of the heavenly Father.

But love entails also a desire for advancement. If our love is actually engrossed with the good of our neighbor, we will be deeply moved by the fact that the other, according to our belief, is the victim of error. We consider this fact regretfully and we endure it reluctantly. This is a painful situation to be endured by *tolerance*. But to endure is not to approve, and our love would not be real if it did not try to help others to attain truth and to pursue good. But it would not be real either if it lost sight of the dignity of the moral subject contained in the person. That is why it uses only the means corresponding to this dignity, such as the example of a life animated by a great love of truth.

Built on the solid foundation of love, human coexistence needs, moreover, a juridical order ratifying the prescriptions of justice.

As an appreciation of the other person and as a desire for betterment, love consitutes a direct relation of person to person: my love is applied directly to the person of my neighbor and, if there is reciprocity, my person is the immediate end of his love. That is why love is defined as a direct relation of subject to subject, as a subjective relationship.

Nevertheless, if in the order of intention love is directed toward the neighbor, in the order of realization it attains it effectively only through the medium of objective elements, and, therefore, through objective relationships. The reason for this is that its consitutive elements — appreciation and desire for betterment — remain enclosed within us as long as we do not embody them in objective relationships. Our disposition in regard to others will remain purely interior, if we do not reveal it to them by signs: a smile, a gesture of approval, a word of encouragement, an act of kindness, a gift, etc. are, in fact, material elements, but which take on a deeply human meaning as soon as they become the means of expression for an encounter in the mutual esteem of love.

Love will miss its purpose if it is not expressed by acts or outward services which bring real help to another. The subjective relationship that constitutes love must, therefore, be embodied in some objective elements and, by that very fact, it is the source and the end of objective relationships. This implication of subjective and objective relations reflects our manner of being. We are incarnate spirits. Just as the objective elements which constitute our body are animated by spiritual interiority whose intentions they express, so our subjective relations vitalize our objective relations and develop into them.

The indispensable role of the objective elements in our coexistence places us at the heart of justice, the principal virtue in the sphere of objective relations. For a long time moralists have affirmed that justice included an objective element — *medium rei* — and created, therefore, some objective relations.

Before considering what the order of justice in the domain of objective relations consists in, it is necessary beforehand to consider why these relations require the realization of a particular order which maintains them in their role in the service of subjective relations.

First of all the necessity for this order arises from the appropriate character of the material elements included in the objective relations. Spiritual values are indivisible and inexhaustible. Everyone can share in them without their being lessened or without the participation of one hindering that of another. Thousands of scientists can be interested in the same science; their scientific knowledge can progress continually and, far from being an obstacle to each other, each one of them can enrich all the others by communicating to them his personal discoveries while not diminishing anything of his own knowledge. What is more, their common participation in the same spiritual values is of such a nature as to create among them a spiritual kinship and a communion in which the mutual exchange of personal experience promotes the scientific knowledge of each and every one of them. By their very essence, spiritual values unite those who participate in them, and conflicts in the spiritual domain are able to spring only from involuntary errors or from the bad dispositions of men. We are not able to say as much of the material elements of our objective relations. Material goods must be divided in order that several may share them, and the share of each one becomes less insofar as the number of participants increases. Partial or complete use of a good by an individual excludes the partial or total simultaneous use by another. Therefore, it is from the very nature of material goods that conflicts are able to originate. There is, for example, the conflict of interest between the farmer cultivating his land and the State intending to make use of the land for the construction of a road. It will be necessary then to foresee an order so as to anticipate or resolve their conflicts. It is obvious that this order will always become more complicated considering that cultural progress, especially scientific and technical, involves in a more and more intense way a continually growing quantity of material goods in human relations. Let us take as an example transportation. Now, it is obvious that a more and more complicated and strict order is established to regulate traffic of greater proportions. To be convinced of it, it suffices to think of the extensive traffic regulations: a century ago everyone would have ridiculed this group of laws which today are a vital necessity.

But the necessity of an order appropriate to the objective relations does not depend only on the nature of the material goods; it results also from the situation of the subjects which are engaged in it.

Man can abuse his freedom and fail in his duties of love in coexistence with others. If he lets himself be guided by his egoism, his objective relationships, instead of having love as their beginning and end, will serve as a means of procuring advantages and pleasures at the expense of others. In order to save the human values of coexistence an established order will be necessary, exercising the necessary restraint to protect the human meaning of objective relationships from the evil dispositions of those who violate them in bad faith.

But even if everybody were always in good faith, an effective order would still be necessary to protect the objective relations arising from coexistence. Indeed, we are limited and fallible, subject to ignorance and error. It may be as a consequence that by following in good faith an erroneous conscience, we are getting involved in some objective relations prejudicial to life in society. This is another reason for which it is necessary to impose an order in objective relations so that we will fulfill our obligations as social beings when, in spite of ourselves, we may leave them undone.

The requisite elements are arranged in such a way as to determine the necessity and the object as much of justice as of the juridical order which guarantees its practice. *Justice has as object the totality of indispensable objective relations in the realization of love.* In other words, the object of justice is the essential minimum of objective relations without which the recognition of man by man becomes impossible. Now, in order that each person be treated according to his dignity as a human subject, everyone must be faithful to the objective relations placed on them in their condition as social beings. Consequently, *justice has for its object all the objective relations required for life in society, namely, for coexistence. collaboration and coparticipation.* From the point of view of coexistence, respect for the dignity of fundamentally equal persons and groups of persons requires equality in interchanges which constitutes the object of commutative justice. In collaboration each one must furnish a contribution in proportion to his capacities; this is the object of legal justice. Coparticipation demands that the community, represented by those who exercise authority, function in such a way that each one may be able to attain the function suitable to his actual possibilities (which is at the same time a requirement of collaboration), and that all may share in the fruits of the collaboration according to their needs; this belongs to distributive justice.

Some people say that the juridical order is indispensable because man is a threat to the personal dignity of his neighbor — homo homini lupus — and that law and justice would have no reason for existing in a perfect communion of love.[24] This thesis ignores the complexity of reasons for which our objective relations cannot do without a juridical order. Without doubt, this order is indispensable for forcing those who are ill-disposed to submit to the demands of these relations in spite of their bad will. Let it not be forgotten that the objective relations are equally in need of the juridical order in virtue of the very nature of the material elements which are implied there and because of the fact that the persons who are engaged in it, regardless of their good faith and their right intentions, can be cheated in following their erroneous conscience.

It is important to note that the object of justice and, consequently, of the juridical order is not a static and unalterable principle. Assuredly, it presents a static aspect in this sense that it is expressed by a totality of rules which represent a certain level of requirements below which a society could not agree to descend. But we may not forget so long as justice is a dynamic virtue that its content is progressive and must be enriched constantly.

On the one hand, this progress is conditioned by the level of subjective culture, notably, by the degree of moral education. Insofar as someone is better prepared to know and put into practice the requirements of the recognition of man by man, he becomes more sensitive to the objective elements which he must include in his relationships with others in order to treat them as persons. Historically we can state that the great figures in the social domain, under the inspiration of an inventive love, have enriched objective relations with new values which later have inspired the development of the juridical order. That is why we can say that justice represents in civilization the present level of the work already accomplished by charity.

On the other hand, the progress of culture continually adds to the quantity of available goods and increases proportionally the minimum of objective elements indispensable in just relationships. What at a given moment, in view of the level of culture already attained, becomes *socially* possible, falls by that very fact under the requirements of justice. How, in fact, would we dare to claim that in the life of a social group we respect the dignity of the human persons if we neglect to enrich the relations with the help of the possibilities which we have at our disposal for the good of all? It would not be difficult to substantiate these considerations by having recourse to quite a few of the elements of social legislation, and to show that justice is a dynamic reality with progressive contents whose object evolves with the progress of culture and the recognition of man by man. Besides, considering that justice has its beginning and end in love, it is not astonishing that it participates in the dynamism of love.

We have said that love, the foundation of all human co-existence, determines how we have to conduct ourselves with regard to freedom of conscience in our person-to-person relationships. But love alone does not suffice in regulating coexistence. As the latter is a structure of objective relations, it needs juridical order, sanctioning the demands of justice. To what extent can and must authority, qualified as regards the juridical order, impose restrictions on freedom of conscience in virtue of justice?

In order to uphold the truly human value of the coexistence of those under its jurisdiction, the first element of the common good, authority must prevent the exercise of freedom of conscience from impairing the rights of others. A few examples will illustrate this principle. In certain countries a large number of citizens proclaim the legitimacy of segregation and racial discrimination. If they act according to this conviction, they will perpetrate unjust actions toward those whom they consider as belonging to an inferior race. The legislator in no way oversteps the limits of his jurisdiction by compelling them to respect in their objective relations all the measures required to assure the civic equality of all citizens. In the same manner, he will have to impose the observance of· the demands of tolerance on the one who is convinced that the beliefs to which he adheres urge him to be against the freedom of those who are of another opinion. He will have to prevent the violent acts of a militant atheist, who is convinced that he is practicing virtue by wiping out all religion. He will have to curb the freedom of those who think they have the right to bring about direct abortion for the planning of births. Indeed, the first personal right to be respected in human coexistence is the right of life. If the legislator does not forbid abortion, he neglects to protect the basic right to life, and this negligence is all the more serious as it is a question of human lives which do not yet have the capacity to defend themselves.[25]

In all these cases — and we could mention many others — it is a question of the most urgent requirement of the common good: in order to assure the human character of coexistence, the juridical order must protect personal rights against every injustice. This very classic principle is adopted in the treatises on justice when they affirm that the authority of the State must protect the citizens against unjust aggressors, whether they make an attempt in bad faith against the rights of others (formally unjust aggression) or if they act in good faith (materially unjust aggression). What is true on the level of the State is of equal value on the international level: in order to rise to its most elementary task, the authority of the international society must make use of sufficiently efficacious means to keep a government from encroaching upon the rights of citizens, of minorities, of other States included in international coexistence.

We can conclude that the first element of the common good, namely, the basic set of requirements of life in society requires as many restrictions in the exercise of freedom of conscience as are necessary to safeguard the rights of each and everyone.[26]

But authority still has to exercise another function in the area of coexistence: its mission includes a pedagogical aspect. St. Thomas said that it has to promote the virtuous life of those under its jurisdiction. In other words, it must be concerned with the level of public morality, determined by the conduct of persons and groups. But, in this connection, it is necessary not to neglect the restrictions that wisdom and prudence lay down in the name of morality. On the one hand, authority will not tolerate that those people who are not capable of forming their judgment of conscience according to the requirements of values already acquired do harm to the level of morality already socially realized. On the other hand, it will be careful to prescribe measures which are not socially feasible.

To give an example. In certain countries the law forbids the sale of contraceptives or, permitting the sale of them, it outlaws publicizing them. In most cases these laws have been voted by a Catholic majority, which condemns the use of contraceptives because of the natural law. Now, it is a fact that nearly all non-Catholics see no moral evil in them from the moment that these means are utilized in the perspective of a fecundity which in other respects is generous. For them, what is connected with morality are the motives responsible for the regulation of births, while the choice of the means is a purely technical question and will be determined by the degree of effectiveness and by medical and psychological reasons. Also, they claim that Catholics, using legal measures according to their own viewpoint, are exercising an illegitimate restraint on their freedom of conscience since they are denying them legal access to means which they consider morally lawful. It is evident that in our societies in which Catholics and non-Catholics live side by side, the Catholic conception in this matter is not part of what is socially desirable. Then, if it is introduced into legislation, it will probably give birth to a law which will do more harm than good. We do not have the right to question the sincerity of those who claim that freedom of publicity in favor of contraceptives, of their sale and of the activity of institutions teaching their use, is protecting the common good by preventing a number of abortions to which married couples would have recourse so that they could prevent undesired pregnancies. If we consider the staggering number of abortions in our Western countries, we will particularly appreciate the wisdom of St. Thomas who rejects in the name of morality laws which, under the pretext of idealism, bring about greater evils than they prevent. The rejection of contraceptive contrivances is neither socially realized nor feasible. From the juridical point of view the use of these devices must be considered as a private affair. Since freedom of conscience has to be respected as much as possible, Catholics should not resort to legal procedures to forbid access to devices whose use is not considered wrong by non-Catholics.

This freedom does not prevent Catholics from conforming to their conscience: tolerance concerning the sale of contraceptives obliges no one to buy them or to use them.[27]

The same attitude of tolerance seems worthwhile for Catholics from the point of view of international coexistence.

Thought has been given to whether Catholics should not insist that aid be given to countries in the process of development only on condition that they exclude all contraceptive propaganda from the demographic policy. We can only admire the understanding of the great President of the United States, John F. Kennedy, who repeatedly stressed that the obligation of rich countries to grant assistance to countries in the process of devolopment cannot be restricted because of the nature of the demographic policy followed by the countries who have to decide for themselves the policy most likely to serve their own interests.

Wealthy countries must assure countries which are in the development stage the aid sufficient for their social and economic progress in such a way that, if they wish, they may draw from their own revenues the resources necessary for their demographic policy. Besides, under these same principles, Catholics will try to induce the authority of the international society to require developing countries, besides all others, to banish from their demographic policy the practice of abortion, an offense against the right of life, incompatible with human coexistence.

B. The Requirements of Collaboration

We distinguish in culture a subjective aspect and an objective aspect. By subjective culture we understand the development of the different possibilities of the human person, notably, his scientific formation, the refinement of his artistic taste, the promotion of his health, his moral perfection, etc. Objective culture includes the totality of our production brought about by our work in the world, such as science, technology, art, economic goods, language, social institutions, political and juridical order, international organization, etc. Between objective and subjective culture there exists a dialectic relation, an exchange by which one calls on the other and they influence each other mutually. Subjective culture, even in its most spiritual aspects, is not able to spread without the assistance of the values of objective culture: no scienctific formation without books or laboratories, no esthetic life without works of art, no physical culture without material goods; in short, we must utilize the goods of objective culture in order to make them useful in our plans of personal perfection and development. In its own way, the progress of subjective culture is the source of new realizations in the domain of objective culture.

As soon as someone has been formed by contact with the characteristics of the objective culture of his milieu he can, by virtue of his original talents and according to his personal capacities, enrich in his turn the objective culture with new acquisitions. To develop himself, man must, therefore, humanize and transform the universe into a world of objective culture which, in its turn, forms him and helps him to perfect himself more and develop himself according to new dimensions. It could be said that "man fulfills himself while fulfilling the universe." [28]

Yesterday's objective culture is the source of today's subjective culture, and the latter is at the starting point for the enrichment of tomorrow's objective culture. In that way, the reciprocity, through time, between objective culture and subjective culture makes culture a reality with historical dimensions.

But this uninterrupted reciprocity is also a social occurrence. Why is culture necessarily a social reality, a fruit of collaboration?

To perfect our subjective culture we need a great diversity

of values, such as economic goods, science, technology, art, etc. No one is sufficient to realize in himself alone all the goods requisite for a truly human subjective culture. This insufficiency results, first of all, from our temporality: our acts are subject to temporal succession and for lack of time we are not able to realize all that we need. But temporality is not the only limitation on our possibilities. We have already said that each person is an originality. Each one possesses human possibilities, individually limited. This limitation of our aptitudes and our capacities is shown by a need for assistance. Where will this help come from? We must expect it from each other. Indeed, our originality expresses not only the fact of our limitation, it shows also that each one is limited in his own way, different from others because of his individual talents. All differ because of their constitution, their temperament, their capacities and from these initial talents all stand out as unique personalities with particular characteristics. This diversity makes us responsive to each other and makes us complete each other. The difference in persons is the source of a wide range of activities, professions and specialties which all contribute to one or other aspect of culture. Thanks to our diversity, we are called to collaborate in the creation of different elements of the objective culture, so that the fruits of collaboration put everyone within reach of a truly human subjective culture. The assertion is paradoxical, but it contains a profound truth: what unites us in social life is not so much what we have in common as what distinguishes us and differentiates us. Clearly our innate equality is an indispensable condition for our collaboration in society. Without it we would not be able to interest ourselves in the same values: collaboration presupposes exactly the encounter with the same values. But the real cause of acting in common is our diversity. That is what unites us and constitutes the source of the rewards of collaboration. We say that a nomad people is primitive because it does not make use of an abundant variety of professions and activities whose function is the realization of the diversity of cultural goods. The cultural level of a people is enriched insofar as its members develop their original and personal talents and spread out their activity in a wide variety of professions, even specialties.

These thoughts allow us to determine the meaning of social life as collaboration and, consequently, to depict the aspect of the common good which is well-founded in the requirements of collaboration.

To accomplish this, we must take into account two important facts. We said that culture is a creation of human work. By work we understand not only the effort devoted to economic production, but all human activity contributing to cultural progress. Now, the first fact to be taken into consideration is that, on the one hand, all persons engaged in coexistence perpetually have needs; on the other hand, all are not able to contribute at the same time to collaboration for the purpose of satisfying these needs. It follows that the active part of every society, which is solely capable of collaborating in the realization of cultural values, has the duty of making sure that the needs of all members are satisfied, including those who lack the ability to share in the common effort. Therein lies a vital demand of our existence. The life of children begins in total dependence on the parents. It would not reach its full development, an essential condition for participation in collaboration, if for several years the activity of the parents were not relieving the total inadequacy of the children. At the end of their youth, the children are grown enough to take an active share in the maintenance of the family beside the parents. But hardly have they arrived at maturity when their parents cross the threshold of old age and have more and more need of their help. Therefore, it is only during a part of our life that we are capable of collaborating actively in the societies to which we belong. What is more, it would be impossible for us to take on a task if, previously, we had not received from others the assistance indispensable for our personal development.

Each one must in turn give himself to others according to his capacities and receive according to his needs the results of the work of others. *This alternate receiving and giving is a fundamental law of all human society.*

The application of this fundamental law requires that the activity of those who are capable of work satisfies the needs of all, including those who are unable to contribute at a given time to collaboration, such as children, the sick, invalids, elderly people, etc. Furthermore, since the reward of this collaboration has its source in the diversity of those who are involved in it, it is necessary that each may be able to live in the way which befits his aptitudes and that he is provided with work which he can do. In Marxist literature we endlessly come across this maxim: Each one according to his capabilities. That those who are able to work use their capabilities to the fullest in the accomplishment of their task is a requirement for acting in common and, besides, it is only basically a repetition of what St. Paul wrote to the Thessalonians: "The charge we gave you on our visit was that the man who refuses to work must be left to starve" (II Thess. 3:10). The aspect of the common good that comprises the totality of the requirements of collaboration is expressed fundamentally in this double obligation of justice: on the one hand, society has to mobilize available resources so that all may develop and grow according to their original talents in order to be formed and prepared for the task which corresponds to their aptitudes (distributive justice); on the other hand, it must take measures likely to stimulate each one to furnish his contribution to collaboration according to his personal capacities (legal justice).

There is another fact which we must consider in order to understand the whole scope of the requirements of collaboration. If it is true that our originality and, consequently, our diversity are the source of collaboration and of its fecundity, it follows that the society which meets the demands of our social being is the universal community of humanity as such. In fact, it alone includes in a conspicuous way all the diversity of individuals, all the various possibilities of different nations. Moreover, the goods of this world by means of which we have to develop the values of objective culture are distributed differently between the regions of the globe. Each country has at its disposal its own natural resources, each territory contains different reserves. It is only by exploiting all these resources in universal collaboration that the common cultural work can exert its fecundity. Actually, worldwide exchanges and contacts have freed nations from their extreme remoteness from one another and from their forced isolation. As a matter of fact, the economy has become international in such a way that a country is on a downward path if it is not successful in planning its national economy so as to adapt to the demands of the world market. What is true in the field of economy is just as true in scientific areas: the progress of science is carried out in universal collaboration, and scientists who are not interested in scientific research undertaken in other countries are hopelessly lagging behind. If nowadays we speak so much of cultural exchanges, it is because we recognize the need of collaboration on a universal scale in order to accomplish our cultural mission. The world has become one unit, and humanity constitutes a totality whose members are included in a universal collaboration.

The requirements of collaboration, being a constitutive element of the common good, must be imposed, even if for that purpose some restrictions in the exercise of freedom of conscience prove to be necessary.

Questioned on the purpose of their work or of their profession, people ordinarily answer that it is their livelihood, the means of assuring sustenance for their family. Without any doubt, work has this signification: elementary justice requires that the one who contributes to collaboration may share in its benefits. However, the first signification of work is that of being a social service. And it is at this exact point that a profession whose services are no longer valued in society is condemned to disappear, because it ceases by that very fact to be a means of livelihood. Since work is essentially a social service, each inididual has precisely the obligation of engaging in it according to his capacities (obligation of legal justice). Authority has the right to press this obligation, even if it must encroach upon the exercise of freedom of conscience. It is in this way that for those who have the capacity and the possibility for work, it can make of their work a condition necessary for sharing in the fruits of collaboration, and thus exert pressure on those who, convinced that work has meaning only for the individual and because of their private means, think that they are dispensed from it. It is justifiable that the advantages granted by social legislation be connected, as a previous condition, to the will to work in those who have the capacity and the possibility for it.

We have repeatedly declared that diversity is the source of fecundity in collaboration. Besides the diversity of persons and nations, there is also the diversity of regions of the world. Each territory possesses different resources. What is lacking in one territory is found in another. This diversity invites peoples to help each other and mutually complement each other. Culture will become richer and more complete insofar as the contribution of all peoples increases. But we are still today wide of the mark. How many under-developed peoples are still incapable of exploiting the reserves of their territory and of thus taking the place which belongs to them in universal collaboration! It is the duty of rich and developed countries to help them become full partners in international collaboration. This is one of the most important aspects of scientific, technical, economic and financial assistance to countries in the process of development. In order to discharge this duty, rich countries must devote a reasonable share of the national income to it. It might even be necessary that the authority in international society impose on each nation a quota in proportion to this income. Obviously, such a policy contradicts radically the conviction of those who, influenced by a strong conception widespread in the last century, maintain that the right of property is absolute and that their personal incomes are not encumbered by any social obligation. By having them pay taxes, a part of which will be devoted to helping poor countries, authority coerces them into an action which goes contrary to their conviction without going beyond the limits of its competence: it must bring those under its jurisdiction around to fulfilling, in spite of themselves, their obligations as social beings.

Clearly, the measures taken by authority will not go farther than is necessary to safeguard the common good: as much freedom as possible. In a number of countries, for example, compulsory military service is thought of as a contribution required for collaboration in the service of national security. In some of these countries conscientious objectors refusing to do their military service are punished by a penalty of imprisonment. That is overstepping the bounds. Assuredly, if the conscientious objectors were relieved of every form of compulsory service, the way would be open to the profiteers who would not hesitate to feign conscientious objection. But to forestall this abuse, there is no need of going as far as imprisonment. At least in times of peace, it will suffice to assign to the conscientious objectors another service equivalent in duration and difficulties by employing them, for example, within the framework of technical aid furnished to developing countries; in this way they will not be forced into an action contrary to their conscience beyond the strict demands of the common good.

In this same connection, it must be said that it is less serious to prevent someone from placing an act resulting from his erroneous conscience than to compel him to act contrary to it. If the common good is sufficiently guaranteed by the omission of certain actions, we do not have the right to impose measures which require that a person go positively contrary to his conscience by prescribing actions that it condemns. There must be as much obligation as is necessary for the common good, but also as much freedom as possible in the obligation.

C. The Requirements of Coparticipation

The development of the values of objective culture is the immediate end of life in society, but oriented towards an ulterior end — subjective culture or the personal perfection of each and everyone.

The effective realization of our subjective culture depends in the final analysis on our personal choice. In order to promote our scientific culture we have to form ourselves by contact with the inventions and works belonging to the scientific domain; to refine our artistic taste, we have to become personally interested in works of art, etc. The fact of taking to heart or of neglecting our personal perfection depends on our free attitude. That is the strictly subjective element of our destiny in relation to which we are autonomous and irreplaceable.

But this personal task is achievable only on condition of being able to make use of the values indispensable to objective culture. Now, it is our involvement in social life which must put these values within our reach. In fact, the alternation of giving and receiving being the fundamental law of the social life, those who are capable of it have to contribute according to their capabilities to the realization of the values of objective culture, and it is necessary that these values, the results of collaboration, be regulated and distributed in such a way that each and everyone may be within reach of whatever they need to complete as perfectly as possible their subjective culture. To the adage: "for each according to his capacities" we must add: "to each according to his needs," a maxim dear to the Marxists as well, but borrowed literally from the New Testament (Acts 4:35).

Envisaging the demands of the coparticipation of each and everyone, according to his actual needs in the fruits of collaboration, we meet the problems relative to the third aspect of the common good and arising from the domain of distributive justice. This element of the common good, constituted by the requirements of distributive justice, assumes a capital importance in our days. Formerly moral treatises devoted only a few pages to distributive justice. The attainment of cultural goods remained the privilege of a minority. How could anyone be particularly interested in distributive justice, considering that there was so little to be "distributed"? Presently, owing to scientific and technical progress, we are witnessing, at least in the developed countries, an impressive growth in the production of economic goods. These goods are clearly part of human culture, and their realization is all the more urgent as they form the indispensable substructure for making man free and unengaged in order to concern himself with other cultural values. The results of collaboration on objective culture are becoming so abundant that, at the cost of an equitable "distribution," the attainment of cultural values can become actually the "common good," the appanage of each and everyone. In other words, the fecundity of collaboration in the values of objective culture constantly increases the possibilites of promoting more and more the subjective culture of everyone. Now, what in this area becomes socially possible, is imposed *ipso facto* as required by distributive justice. In fact, not to be absorbed with putting the ever-increasing possibilities to use for the good of all is to respect neither the intrinsic sense of objective culture whose purpose is to be of use to subjective culture, nor the signification of the fact that society, composed of human persons, must aspire to their development. Therefore, it is not astonishing that all that we have said concerning the dynamism of justice and its progressive content is applied nowadays in the very first place to distributive justice.

It is this dynamism of distributive justice which determines the new dimensions of what is suitably called the social question. With reference to the social question, we often think too exclusively about the sole concern of salaries. In reality, we began to speak explicitly about the social question when members of the working class, having become aware of their common destiny, joined forces in order to win the place which belongs to them in the social life. But, since then the progress of the developed countries requires that the position of the social problem be on a level with the dynamic elan of distributive justice: the social question is solved only insofar as the citizens not only have the possibility of assuming the task which is suitable for their actual capacities (collaboration), but are able to share in the same way, according to their real needs, in the benefits of collaboration (coparticipation). Inside the State, the social question is not confined, therefore, to the sphere of the interests of a single class; it identifies itself with the problem of the social order to be fulfilled with the good of all members in mind. Nevertheless, this conception is still very narrow. In order to satisfy adequately the current possibilities, the social question is to be placed on a worldwide level, within the range of all mankind. Its fair solution implies the concern of putting all peoples in a state of contributing to universal collaboration and of sharing according to their necessities in the fruits of this collaboration. The problem of distributive justice is rising today on a worldwide scale.

It is again the dynamism of distributive justice which requires that the political democracy also must be a social democracy. Resting on the system of universal suffrage, making provisions for regular and free elections, political democracy finds itself bound to take into account the will of the electors and also to respect their rights. This explains why a number of democratic constitutions explicitly guarantee personal rights and freedoms and why in all cases these rights are acknowledged as the natural foundation of the political regime. However, this recognition of the intangibility of personal rights, while being a condition essential for the respect of the dignity and freedom of the members of the society, is not sufficient to assure for all the exercise of these rights. Try as we may to acknowledge the inviolable character of personal rights intended for goods, property, health, personal culture, etc., the proclamation of these rights, which is adequate for privileged persons having the means of exercising them, remains purely theoretical for those who do not have the means. In order to guarantee positive freedom to all — namely, the actual possibility of personal growth and development — political democracy must be extended and completed by the social democracy. The latter, as a matter of fact, consists in enforcing distributive justice in the social order, that is to say, by functioning in such a way that each one is able to contribute, according to his capacities, to collaboration with the intention of promoting objective culture, and is able to share in the benefits of this collaboration according to the necessities of his subjective culture. Political and social democracy must be united as two principles of a personalist system of government. The first is the spiritual principal of all truly human social life, but it is able to vitalize the whole social body only on condition of being embodied in the social democracy. This same truth could be explained by saying that, in order to be on the level of cultural progress, the statesman, as much on the level of particular States as on the international level, must make use of the increasing possibilities and the progressive demands of distributive justice.

That is what we mean when we speak of current problems of top policy on the level of States and of mankind. We emphasize with good reason that social progress consists precisely in assuring to all the attainment of essential or vital goods without which men are not able normally to pursue the development of their subjective culture.

We will insist, first of all, on the necessity of a policy of full employment. In developed States the problems of regional economy are being given higher priority in order that, as far as possible, all those who are capable of working are able to play their role in collaboration. In the international framework we see more and more clearly that, in order to attain its real purpose, assistance to countries in the process of development must be aimed especially at putting them in a state of participation in universal collaboration.

We will stress next that it is a vital necessity for all to be able to exercise, in a truly human measure, their right to the use of economic goods; this right raises the problem of an equitable reallotment of goods. In countries where they are preoccupied with it, they state that, to a large extent, the evolution of social legislation is guided by concern for a redistribution of the national income better adapted to the needs of all. From the international viewpoint we speak of an economy of assistance on a worldwide scale. We mean that the abundance from production in rich countries must make up for the shortages in poor countries in order to allow all persons to exercise their basic right of participation in a truly human manner.

It is evident that health is one of the most vital goods. All citizens need the scientific and technical protection which is available for their health: whence the question of social medicine, that is, the measures to be taken in order that first rate medicine may be within the reach of all. It is continually one of the main questions of the day in developed countries and which, on the international scale, is expressed in medical aid to countries in the developing stage.

Another essential good is the formation of youth. Distributive justice requires that, according to the possibilities, all children receive a formation consistent with their actual aptitudes. Thus, it is not surprising that, in countries which have the means for it, they insist on the necessity of the democratization of education: they extend education and they diversify it so as to give all children the opportunity to receive the formation corresponding to their particular capacities. For those countries in the process of development, they are obliged to multiply the forms of assistance, not only to assure for all what is called "basic education" but also to introduce progressively all the degrees of specialized education.

These are only the most urgent and essential requirements. By meeting them the responsible persons of top policy on the national or international scale cannot lose sight of the fact that they must be faithful to the dynamism of distributive justice, and that the ideal to be fulfilled consists in the widest possible participation of everyone in *all* the values of objective culture.

Authority, responsible for the safeguarding of the common good and, therefore, also of its principal element composed of the requirements of coparticipation or the obligations of distributive justice, is empowered to take for that purpose all the necessary or useful measures, even if the latter curtail the exercise of freedom of conscience.

There still remains in some countries the policy of the *latifundia*, the concentration of the ownership of land in the hands of the propertied class. Such a regime, by maintaining the subjugation of a large body of tenents legitimately aspiring to become autonomous, weighs heavily on the productivity of the farming sector and prevents a wider participation in the benefits of the national economy. In this case the state is obligated to proceed with the redistribution of the lands, even if this measure must run contrary to the views of a few who are convinced of the absolute character of their right to property.

In order to put the resources of quality medicine within the reach of all, the state is qualified to take all measures necessary for the realization of a true program of social medicine, even if these measures have to collide with the beliefs of some doctors, convinced that freedom of profession includes the sovereign right of fixing fees for it.

Concerning the one who is convinced of the absolute character of the right to property and rejects the social aspect of it, authority has the right to require the payment of taxes, even if the contributions have to be used to facilitate the redistribution of the national income or to help countries in the process of development.

The demands of distributive justice are so imperative that the legislator must consider, in proportion as culture progresses, how the ever-increasing possibilities can and will be put to use in furthering the dynamism of this virtue. This aspect of the common good takes on such importance that we must comply with it even against those who, in good faith perhaps — the education which they received hindering them, for example, from understanding the grounds for legal prescriptions — are not able to approve it.

---

1. *Summa Theol.*, IIa-IIae, q. 58, art. 10, ad 1.
2. *Summa Theol.*, Ia-IIae, q. 90, art. 4. Cf. P. M. Van Overbeke,

Droit et morale. Essai de synthèse thomiste, dans Rev. Thom., t. LVIII,
1958, p. 285-336 and 674-694.
 3. *Summa Theol.,* Iᵃ-IIᵃᵉ, q. 100, art. 8.
 4. *Summa Theol.,* Iᵃ-IIᵃᵉ, q. 93, art. 3, ad 3: "Hoc ipsum quod lex
humana non se intromittit de his quae dirigere non potest, ex ordine legis
aeternae provenit. Secus autem esset, si approbaret ea quae lex aeterna
prohibet."
 5. *Summa Theol.,* Iᵃ-IIᵃᵉ, q. 93, art. 3 et q. 96, art. 2, ad 3.
 6. *Summa Theol.,* Iᵃ-IIᵃᵉ, q. 96, art 2, ad 3.
 7. *Summa Theol.,* Iᵃ-IIᵃᵉ, q. 96, art. 2.
 8. *Summa Theol.,* Iᵃ-IIᵃᵉ, q. 96, art. 2.
 9. *Summa Theol.,* IIᵃ-IIᵃᵉ, q. 59, art. 2, ad 1.
 10. *Summa Theol.,* Iᵃ-IIᵃᵉ q. 91, art. 4.
 11. *Summa Theol.,* Iᵃ-IIᵃᵉ q. 96, art. 2, ad 2.
 12. *Summa Theol.,* Iᵃ-IIᵃᵉ q. 100, art. 8.
 13. *De reg. princ.,* l. I, c. 4.
 14. *Summa contra Gent.,* l. III, c. 129.
 15. *Summa contra Gent.,* l. III, c. 128; *Summa Theol.,* Iᵃ-IIᵃᵉ q. 99,
art. 2.
 16. *Summa Theol.,* Iᵃ-IIᵃᵉ q. 98 art. 1; q. 96, art. 3.
 17. *Summa Theol.,* Iᵃ-IIᵃᵉ q. 96, art. 3, ad 2.
 18. *Summa Theol.,* Iᵃ-IIᵃᵉ, q. 92, art. 2, ad 4, et q. 95, art. 1,
 19. *Summa Theol.,* Iᵃ-IIᵃᵉ, q. 96, art. 2, ad 2.
 20. *Quodlibet II,* q. 5, art. 10, ad 2; *Summa Theol.,* Iᵃ-IIᵃᵉ, q. 95,
art. 1; q. 96, art. 2, ad 2; q. 97, art. 1.
 21. J. Dabin, *La philosophie de l'ordre juridique positif,* Paris, 1929,
p. 191 and 627-628. Cf. G. Ripert, *La règle morale dans les obligations
civiles,* Paris, 1935.
 22. It is on the dignity of the moral subject as a human person that
rests what it is suitable to call the "principle of subsidiarity." The expression is not exactly the best one because it expresses neither clearly nor
completely the personalist requirement which it intends to proclaim.
 23. J. Schmid, *Das Evangelium nach Matthäus übersetzt und
erklärt,* Regensburg 4th edition, 1959, p. 148, affirms that the "golden
rule" is found in substance in: *Tob.,* IV, 15; Homère, *Odyssée,* 5, 188
and following; Thalès; in India; in China (Laotse and Kung Futse); in
Islam.
 24. W. Luypen, *Existentiele fenomenologie,* Utrecht, 1959, p. 233.
 25. We are not speaking here of criminal abortion (all non-medical
direct abortion) which the law forbids. Practically all non-Catholics ask
that the law not forbid medical abortion. The case in which it would be
necessary to choose between the life of the mother and that of the child
is becoming more and more theoretical. But there are cases — certain cases
of uraemia, for example — in which, if pregnancy is not interrupted, the

mother dies before the foetus is capable of an extra-uterine life. In these cases it is not possible to save the child and, therefore, it is not a question of choosing between the life of the mother and that of the child. If we refrain from intervening, non-Catholics object that we are guilty of an *omission* which is opposed to technical progress which allows for the saving of at least one life, the mother's, in cases where otherwise both mother and child are destined to die. They say that they only hasten the death of the child who will die anyway even if they do not intervene, and that the idea of abortion does nothing more than this. It is not for the legislator to side with either opinion; it is sufficient that he forbid criminal abortion.

26. By virtue of its pedagogical role, authority can exercise a substitutional function by making certain decisions in place of the subjects in order to protect them from their own ignorance, imprudence or negligence. In this way authority can make insurance against sickness and infirmity obligatory for the economically insecure who do not have the means of taking care of the risks and charges which may arise and who, left to their own devices, would take no further interest in their welfare or that of their family. It is not a violation of a man's freedom if he is prevented from doing harm to himself.

27. F.Suarez, *Tractatus de legibus et legislatore Deo*, 1. I, c. 15, in *Opera omnia*, éd. cit., t. V, p. 60-63, distinguishes prescriptive laws (*praeceptum, lex affirmativa*) and prohibitive (*prohibitio, lex negativa*) from permissive laws (*permissio*). As for the latter, he distinguishes ulteriorly the negative permission, when it is a question of objects about which the law makes no mention (it is the absence of laws in the area of certain bad actions), and the permission properly so-called (*permissio simpliciter dicta*), when the law explicitly states that certain actions will not be punished (by way of example, he cites the law which, while forbidding murder, allows a husband to kill his wife when he catches her in the very act of adultery). 1.) *Positive and negative laws* expressing a precept or a prohibition can never be in opposition to the requirements of morality. In fact, a human lawmaker has no power to impose actions which God forbids; the juridical order arises from the moral order and therefore cannot contradict it: lex iniusta vel turpis non est lex (F. Suarez, *op. cit.*, lib. III, c. 12, p. 215-222). A Catholic will never be able to vote for a law which will call for acts forbidden by morality. If, for example, in reference to a policy dealing with population, a law was proposed to the voters which would prescribe abortion (after, for example, the third pregnancy), it would be immoral to vote for such a law). 2.) *Negative permission* for evil is inevitable to a certain degree. In other words, it is impossible to make prohibitive laws concerning all bad acts. For Saint Thomas, the impossibility of forbidding all evil lies within the domain of *tolerance*. He says that we have to tolerate certain bad things so as not to

cause greater evils or in order that we may not prevent the realization of certain more importaint good things and circumstances. He refers to Saint Augustine who was convinced that, taking into account the moral situation of his time, the prohibition of prostitution would have brought about greater evils: "Aufer meretrices de rebus humanis, turbaveris omnia libidinibus" (*De Ordine*, 1. II, c. 4). Saint Thomas asserts that for the same reasons we will often have to tolerate the religion of non-Christian communities: "ad aliquod malum vitandum, sc. ad vitandum scandalum, vel dissidium quod ex hoc posset provenire, vel impedimentum salutis eorum qui paulatim sic tolerati convertuntur ad fidem" (*Summa Theol.*, IIa-IIae, q. 10, art. II). In our time, the question is more complex. First of all, we distinguish more carefully between the spiritual and the temporal and we say that the legislator must confine himself to the temporal. As far as natural law is concerned, Catholics and non-Catholics, even though they are on the same cultural level, sometimes have different viewpoints. Let them consider a judgment concerning the use of contraceptives. It is not for the legislator to nullify this question in one way or another. Let him refrain from including such matters in the law! 3.) *Permission properly so-called* brings up equally delicate questions. The legislator must forbid deliberate abortion, but must he not make exception for strictly therapeutic abortion? Outside of the Catholic Church, medical abortion is considered lawful by practically everyone. The legislator must proclaim the stability of marriage, but can he not permit divorce in certain strictly defined cases, considering that outside of the Catholic Church general opinion is against absolute *external* indissolubility (that is, they generally agree to the internal indissolubility — the marriage couple does not have the right to dissolve their marriage themselves — but they claim that for grave reasons the dissolution can be provided for in the law, that is, externally, by the legislator)? As far as permissive laws are concerned, must not Catholics be tolerant to the degree that these laws, while respecting the freedom of others, do not encroach upon their freedom? A permission is not an order and the law does not require that whatever is allowed must be done.

28. J. Mouroux, *Sens chrétien de l'homme*, Paris, 1945, p. 12.

CHAPTER 6

RELIGIOUS FREEDOM

Religious freedom is only a matter of applying freedom of conscience. In fact, it is freedom on the one hand for individuals to profess a personal religious faith in conformity with their conviction of conscience, and freedom on the other hand for their religious communities to put this conviction into practice and make use of the means which are indispensable for that purpose. As for every manifestation of freedom of conscience, the decisive elements here are the dignity of the *moral subject* which is the human person and his condition as a *social being*.

Although governed by the same fundamental principles as other expressions of freedom of conscience, religious freedom has a right to a special study. The first reason for this is that the religious conviction of the human person contains what is most essential for the fundamental choice which he is called upon to make and which conditions the basic trend of his whole existence. Therefore, in this domain more than in any other the prerogatives of the person as a moral subject will have to be carefully considered. But there is above all a second reason, the fact that through their conviction the persons are affiliated with religious communities, living according to traditions considered as sacrosanct, even made known directly or indirectly by God. The situation is all the more delicate because these communities will claim that, far from being subject to other societies, it belongs to them to determine by their intangible principles the comportment of their adherents, including their social relations.

This second reason is particularly applicable to us Catholics. We believe that our religion is revealed and supernatural; therefore, as to its origin and its content it is divine. According to a formula dear to the Greek Fathers — summarizing, also, a magnificent text of St. Paul (Tit. 3:3-7) — *all* come *from* the Father, *through* the Son, *in* the Holy Spirit. The Father is charity (agape), and He shows this love in the world in a visible and tangible way by the incarnation of His own Son (I John 4:8-10) and by His death for us, sinners and enemies of God (Romans 5:6-11). We all come then from the Father, from His initiative. The Son is the Mediator: it is through Him that the Father communicates everything to us. Being God made man, the Son is the sacrament, the visible and efficacious sign through whose intervention the love of the Father has come into the world. Beyond His glorification, which is shielded from the eyes of men, He continues to live in the Church which He founded Himself and which remains the sacrament, the efficacious sign by which the love of the Father must spread and progress in us until it reveals His complete triumph, when the Father will be all in all (I Cor. 15:20-28). Everything comes to us, therefore, through Christ, sole Mediator between the Father and men (I Tim. 2:5). Turned into a living spirit (I Cor. 15:22, 45), the glorifield Lord fulfills effectively in us the gifts of the love of the Father in the Holy Spirit. Indeed, the Holy Spirit is imparted to us in Baptism to diffuse the love of the Father in our hearts (Rom. 5:5); in this way, He makes us children of the Father and, as His children, capable of speaking to Him in our prayers; He lives in us and leads us (Rom. 8:14-16); He has us bear about within us the fruits of a Christian life in charity (Gal. 5:22-25); He helps us accept the Gospel (I Cor. 13:4-5) and increase in the knowledge of the things which God has given us through His grace (I Cor. 2:12); He helps the members of the hierarchy to assure the efficacy of the worship over which they watch and the sacraments which they administer (John 20:21-23); He also helps them in order to guarantee the certainty of the teaching and of the directives which they give us (John 14:15-17, 26; 15:26-27; 16:12-15; Act. 1:5, 8; 2:33). Everything comes to us in the Holy Spirit, principle of our Christian life, soul of the Church.

These divine realities dominate our whole "existence-in-the-world-with-others." This world is not only declining and unstable; it is out of proportion with the new creature that we will become and that we have already become.[1] Although our Christian existence is mingled with the things of the world, the true eternal realities for which we strive determine our attitude and our comportment. In other words, the facts of Christian revelation — the requirements of the love of the Father in which we share, the structure and mission of the Church which Christ has founded, the necessities of Christian life which the Holy Spirit has imparted to us — constitute the norm of our religious existence and the decisive criterion in our relations with those who do not share our conviction. That is why we must ask ourselves, in the light of revelation, how we must act in regard to non-Catholic persons and communities and how, consequently, religious freedom exists in life in society, considered as coexistence, collaboration and coparticipation.

CATHOLICISM AND COEXISTENCE

We have said that love is the essential principle of life in society considered as coexistence. Love respects another in his dignity as a human person, and as a consequence it respects and appreciates the one who, loyally following the judgment of his sincerely formed conscience, although erring in good faith, is faithful to his dignity as a *moral subject*. Love is distressed when a neighbor is in error. It will not compel, it will not force the one who is mistaken to accept the truth, but it will abstain from every means of coercion repugnant to the dignity of the moral subject who is its neighbor. In that way, love guarantees freedom of conscience in coexistence.

When the problem of freedom of conscience is placed in the religious domain, the Catholic faith enriches with new motives the attitude to be taken in regard to the expression of freedom of conscience, or religious fredom. These motives are set up in the light of Catholic dogma concerning the act of faith.

The act of faith is above all the fruit of the grace of God. No one can come to Christ if the Father does not draw him (John 4:44), if this is not by virtue of a gift from the Father (John 6:65). Therefore, no one can impose the faith on another by compulsion. To arrogate to oneself the right of intervening directly would be to put oneself rashly in the place of the influence of His grace. However, our love, if it is a true desire for the conversion of others, will not remain indifferent to the fact that another does not have the Christian faith which constitutes in our eyes an appreciable blessing. Must it, then, remain sterile? St. Paul teaches us the productive and strong attitude that our love has to embrace in order to come to the assistance of those who have no share in the gift of our Christian faith: "I urge, therefore, first of all, that supplication, prayers, intercessions and thanksgivings be made for all men. ... This is good and agreeable in the sight of God our Savior, Who wishes all men to be saved and to come to the knowledge of the truth" (I Tim. 2:1-4). Christ Himself directed us to ask the Father that His name be hallowed, His kingdom come, and His will be done (Matt. 6:9-10). For a Christian, respect for religious freedom is based on his deference towards divine initiative and develops into a prayer imploring the grace of the faith for all mankind.

On man's part the act of faith is an answer to the initiative of God. In order that the divine grace which draws us may become truly ours, it is still necessary that we give our free consent. A faith imposed by compulsion is, therefore, a contradiction in terms, not only from the point of view of the free initiative of God, but also from the free adherence which it assumes is in man. St. Augustine said that man can place acts without willing to do so but he is able to believe, only by willing to do so: *caetera potest homo nolens, credere vero non nisi volens.*[2] St. Thomas repeats the same thing — at least in reference to those who have never had the Christian faith [3] — *quia credere voluntatis est.* For a Christian the faith is the supreme realization of his freedom, because the freedom of being able to respond to the initiative of the grace of God crowns the highest possibilities of his being. Also, his love of neighbor will concentrate his will for the conversion of others on that divine fulfillment of the freedom of the neighbor. It will not appeal to restraint, but it will mobilize every means of the apostolate after the example of Christ, the Apostle par excellence, (missus *a Patre*), Who fulfilled His mission by the example of His life and by the testimony that He made to the truth (John 18: 37) and for which He shed His own blood and not that of others.

Christian dogma which affirms the supernatural and free character of the act of faith is, then, the best guarantee for the respect of religious freedom. That is why the attitude of those — who not only reject all absolute truth and still claim that respect for the freedom of others is possible only by acknowledging relativism — is deeply resented by Catholics as a form of extreme intolerance. We are most certainly convinced of the divine and consequently absolute character of revealed truths. But it is precisely a revealed doctrine — the doctrine asserting in an absolute way the supernatural and free character of the act of faith — which is the basis of our tolerance and which requires from us an attitude of respect and modesty in the sphere of religious freedom.

Therefore, we can conclude that in life in society, envisaged under the aspect of coexistence, respect for religious freedom — outstanding expression of freedom of conscience — is imposed on Catholics, not only because of the love which respects in every human person his dignity as a moral subject, but also as a natural consequence of the revealed doctrine on the very essence of the act of faith.

CATHOLICISM AND COLLABORATION

Since they are in the world (John 17:15) and engaged in the cultural destiny of humanity, Catholics have the obligation of taking an active part in collaboration. On the professional and national level their earthly task places them in contact with citizens who do not share their religious conviction. Moreover, if they are devoted to activities belonging to international life, they are moving necessarily in surroundings still more diversified and disparate. It follows that it is an impossibility for them to avoid cultural collaboration with non-Catholics.

Two reasons determine for a Christian the dignity and grandeur of his participation in the cultural task which is incumbent upon all humanity.

The first is that he knows that he has been created in the image of God (Gen. 1:17). That man is the likeness of God means in the language of the Bible that he is His representative, His "lieutenant." Now, God is the Creator and Lord of His work. As the likeness of God man is, therefore, also the creator and lord of creation in the dependence on and in the service of God. Holy Scripture also adds that God has given him the mission of dominating the earth (Gen. 1.28), of keeping watch over creation and shaping it (Gen. 2:5, 15). In other words, God has put resources and virtualities in the world, and, in man, talents and possibilities which will attain their fullness only by the active vigilance and intervention of man. The image of God, man will fulfill his mission of creator and lord in his rank as second and free cause by transforming more and more the natural environment into a cultural environment and by fulfilling himself by that very fact. If so, work — namely, every activity by which man dominates the earth and brings about culture — takes on a religious signification. The Christian must work in the awareness that he is a co-operator with God (I Cor. 3:9), that the daily task to which he devotes himself is truly an *opus Dei* and that, consequently, the conscious acceptance of religious meaning of his daily work is an essential element of his mission to do all for the glory of God (I Cor. 10:31).

Moreover, the great commandment that Jesus gave to His disciples (Matt. 22:39; John 14:34-35) and to which He will refer as a decisive criterion of judgment (Matt. 25:31-46) is the commandment concerning love of our neighbor. As we have already stressed, the intrinsic and basic meaning of work and of professional activity is that of being a social service. For a Christian, that means that his love, which to be real has to promote the good of others, will be embodied fundamentally in the task which he assumes each day in the midst of the community of men. A Christian who does not take seriously the exercise of his profession is unworthy of his name (Didache 12:3-5) because he is neglecting an important element of the positive practice of charity. He will live, on the contrary, the religious signification of his work if he sees in it the embodiment of the most essential value of Christianity, that is, charity.

These two considerations determine the place of the Christian in the presence of earthly values. First of all, in order to be faithful to the intentions of his Creator, he has to develop his natural talents: revelation in itself does not make him capable of assuming his cultural mission; he must exploit his own human aptitudes in order to respond to the scientific, technical, artistic, and other requirements of his task here below. Next, he must be faithful to the law of love which he received from his Savior: if he lives according to this charity, he will be all the more suited to devoting himself to his cultural task in the service of the community, because the dynamism of his virtue will help him discover and invent increasingly human solutions to cultural problems. Is it not true that, in the course of history, it has been those who were animated by great charity who have improved the conditions in the life of their fellowmen, who have been the source of cultural progress, who have been responsible for better institutions and legislation worthy of the dignity of man?

Therefore, it is a duty for the Catholic to contribute to the cultural task of humanity. But on what basis will his collaboration with non-Catholics be worked out? The cultural domain has its own consistency and its own laws, its methods and its means of action. But as a human reality, it must be governed by the norms of morality. Then, it should not be surprising that the Church, whose mission is to have dogmatic and moral truths penetrate into everyday life, continually teaches its faithful the moral norms which must govern their worldly activities. The moral norms governing the cultural domain arise principally from natural law, that is, from what is demanded by the dignity of the human person. Therefore, their validity can be recognized also by non-Christians and even by atheists. Christians can, as a consequence, present programs of cultural activities in which those who are not Christians or who do not believe in God can find their profound aspirations. In the field of secular values they will be able to communicate by efforts and ideas with all those who, without sharing their faith, are pursuing the realization of a truly human order. It is even possible that they may find some human values better understood among non-Christians than in some Catholic surroundings. It is on this basis of common aspirations and moral norms that collaboration becomes possible.

Besides, the possibility, indeed the necessity, of this collaboration has been stated over and over again by the Church, especially in the social and international domain. The Church has never claimed that she alone can solve the social problem.[4] She exhorts her faithful to collaborate in the social domain with non-Catholics who accept her social doctrine.[5] She declares that collaboration is desirable with all institutions which, in theory and in practice, respect the demands of natural law, even if they do not acknowledge explicitly that God is the Creator and Legislator of the universe.[6] "Certain elementary principles of a moral and religious character exist which constitute the fundamental inheritance of all people and on which there is agreement as on an inevitable foundation for common life, in order to attain the construction of a true social and worldwide order of justice and peace."[7] In other words, the Church accepts and recommends cooperation on the common ground of the decalogue, on the hand, in collaboration with those who believe in the existence of God and, from the second table of the law, on the other hand — commandments concerned with relations among men — in the encounter with those who, without adhering to a religious faith, recognize from a practical viewpoint the objective requirements of the human person.

The basis for collaboration once established, the form which it will take remains to be settled. In a general way we will say that conditions for collaboration must be of such a nature that Catholics are able to remain themselves, that is, safeguard their religious life and accomplish their apostolic mission. It follows that the concrete forms of collaboration will depend on the contingencies of the different practical situations.

When their freedom is respected and when conditions of collaboration are guaranteed which will permit them to be and remain completely themselves, Catholics are not out of place in the setting and organization in which they cooperate with non-Catholics. Such a solution obviously presents the advantage of avoiding isolation: the foundation of organizations according to diversity of convictions is always threatened with the danger of giving rise to the formation of ghettos.

Moreover, the presence of Catholics in disparate groups is a requisite of their apostolic mission. The role of the Christian laymen is, in fact, to be the spiritual ferment in the secular order. They are the Church; and through them the Church must be the principle of the life of human society.[8] Besides, this form of close collaboration in the midst of groups or organizations presupposes the realization of indispensable conditions: the more Catholics mix with others, the more they will need to reinforce their religious conviction and their apostolic spirit; the more also will they need the protection of projects and associations of a religious nature to keep up their Christian and apostolic spirit. It is not suprising that Catholic Action, the contemporary form of the influence of the Church in the world, is in the first place a school of formation for the Christian conscience, necessary to prepare for a bold and creative collaboration.

When, on the contrary, the partners have no respect for the freedom of Catholics or, in their activities, they proclaim principles, pursue objectives or adopt methods with which Catholics cannot agree, collaboration within the framework of these organizations would create an equivocal situation, and the presence of Catholics would only serve to increase the credit or the influence of the organizations in which Catholics could actually do nothing. In these cases they must do their best to arrange themselves in groups in the center of secular life. In doing this, they are not isolating themselves or seeking the life of a recluse: this would be opposed to their mission in the world. But they join forces in order to be and remain themselves, and this is, on their part, a normal and necessary thing. They are not disassociating themselves from others; they are seeking, on the contrary, in the midst of their own groups, an increase of efficiency and solidarity in order to make their contribution to temporal activity. Moreover, if collaboration in a permanent fashion is not possible, they should cooperate with others each time that the precise objectives of the matter do not call into question the principles of their faith and their morality.

It is necessary to guard against dealing with this problem of the forms of collaboration in too simple a way and of bringing to it a radical solution concerning single principles. Studies in sociology and social psychology urge prudence and sharpen the sense of shades of meaning. In certain cases, it is stated that the fact of grouping together on the basis of a common conviction supports the dynamism of collaboration with others, while in other cases it leads to the isolation of an exclusive group. According to psychological dispositions, the existence of a plurality of organizations within the same area of cultural activities is the source, either of oppositions and sterile conflicts, or of a healthy and beneficial competition.

In some countries where democratic freedoms are not menaced, it will sometimes be better not to carry to extremes organizations based on the difference of conceptions of life in the world in order to ward off isolation and to ghettoism, by contrast, in authoritarian or totalitarian regimes the presence of strong groups, in no way disposed to support organizations which oppose the concepts which animate them, will constitute a protection against the ideological intrusion of the state. These findings show that the forms and modalities of collaboration depend on contingencies. It is necessary to be aware of it in order to be constantly disposed to re-examining one's positions and asking within one's conscience what solution is the best in a particular situation in order to promote collaboration in cultural values.

In all cases Catholics can never forget that their faith and their charity oblige them to participate in collaboration, but also to follow paths and methods consonant with loyal and fruitful contribution.

CATHOLICISM AND COPARTICIPATION

We have said that coparticipation of each and everyone in the goods of objective culture is a requirement of distributive justice. The principal objective of social legislation consists precisely in "distributing" to all, according to their actual needs, the fruits of collaboration. There can be no distinction between citizens based on their convictions. It is obvious that, in the last instance, each one must be able to share in the benefits of life in society because he has needs.

In the sphere of *social* legislation, no one thinks of treating unequally the members of society on the basis of their religious conceptions. This legislation came into existence only recently and it is expanding in a social climate favorable to freedom of conscience and religious freedom. But does not the *civil* law, elaborated in the course of a very long tradition, still carry a few prejudices belonging to the past? In some countries are not Catholics tempted to hold on to certain privileges? These privileges find their explanation, perhaps, in the context of laws reflecting the historical situations in which they were granted, but they no longer fit in with the contemporary mentality which is sensitive about the dignity of each human person whatever his religious opinion may be. The civil law is part of the cultural objective too. By this title it has to assure an identical status to all for the simple reason that all need the guarantee of a juridical order.

It is sometimes said that, in its relations with temporal societies, the Catholic Church has the right to claim a privileged position because it professes the only true faith and only truth has rights. But is not this argument based on an ambiguity? In the appropriate sense of the terms, truth has no rights. What we must say — we have not ceased repeating it — is that we have obligations connected with truth, that is, we must do our best to conform our conscience to the requirements of objective truth. But the essence of rights is, on the one hand, the human person as a moral subject and, on the other hand, societies as groups of *persons* called to defend and promote the good of *human persons*.

If all members, by the very virtue of their quality as citizens, must have a concern in the same statute established by civil law, how must temporal societies — national or internation — intervene in the domain of religious freedom in order to remain faithful to their essence and their mission?

Temporal Societies and Religious Freedom

Pagan antiquity did not distinguish temporal society from the religious community. Temporal life and religious life were merged in the structure of a single and unique society and governed by one political authority. Christ put an end to this confusion of domains by imparting to His Church the realities of revelation in order to engender, develop and direct the religious life of the faithful. Since then, States — as well as international societies — have been confined to the temporal domain. It follows that authority in temporal societies is not qualified to be the judge in the area of religious truth. It would overstep the limits of its jurisdiction if it arrogated to itself the right to decide on the truth or error of different religions. That is why it is not qualified to elaborate a legal statute proclaiming a specific religion — for example, the Catholic religion — the religion of the State. By doing this it would dictate to those under its jurisdiction a religious conviction to which they would have to adhere in order to remain within the law, and, in this way, it would impose an imperative judgment in a matter which is not within its scope.

If authority in temporal societies is unqualified to intervene directly in the religious domain as such, it has, however, a mission to fulfill in regard to those whom it governs: it *must* govern them as persons, that is to say, by respecting their dignity as moral subjects. Now, as a moral subject the person can meet the requirements of his relationship to God only by faithfully following the judgment of his conscience by means of which he sincerely thinks that he understands those requirements. It is on this dignity of moral subject that religious freedom is grounded, the freedom to act in conformity with the religious conviction to which one loyally adheres. In order to acknowledge and protect effectively the dignity of moral subjects in their members, temporal societies — States or international society — must, therefore, sanction religious freedom in their legislation.

From the international point of view religious freedom has been proclaimed explicitly by the *Universal Declaration of*

Human Rights, adopted by the General Assembly of the United Nations on December 10, 1948. Article 18 of this Declaration stipulates: "Everyone has the right to freedom of thought, conscience and religion; this right includes the freedom to change his religion or belief, and freedom, either alone or in community with others and in public or private, to manifest his religion or belief in teaching, practice, worship and observance." Article 30 of this same Declaration stresses that under no pretext can an individual or community violate religious freedom — as well as other rights and freedoms stated in the Declaration: "Nothing in this Declaration may be interpreted as implying for any State, group or person any right to engage in any activity or to perform any act aimed at the destruction of any of the rights and freedoms set forth herein." This proclamation of religious freedom approaches very closely what John XXIII wrote in his Encyclical *Pacem in terris*: "Every human being has the right to honor God according to the dictates of an upright conscience, and the right to profess his religion privately and publicly." Just as the preamble of the Declaration proclaimed its faith "in the fundamental rights of man, in the dignity and value of the human person," so the Pope numbers religious freedom among those rights of man which he calls universal, inviolable, and inalienable (*quae, ut generalia et inviolabilia sunt, ita mancipari nullo modo possunt*) and suited to man in virtue of his dignity as a person. The differences between the two formulations are of rather an incidental nature. The Declaration simply places freedom of conscience and religious freedom side by side, while John XXIII notes that freedom of conscience includes religious freedom by being an application of it. The Pope is satisfied to state in a general way that freedom of conscience extends to the private and public profession of the religion to which one adheres in conscience. The Declaration makes this profession more explicit by specifying that it can be made individually or in community and can be manifested by teaching, practices, worship and rites. The Declaration speaks of the freedom of changing religion or conviction, while John XXIII limits himself to declaring in a general way that in a religious matter one has the right to follow his sincerely formed conscience, *ad rectam conscientiae suae normam* (according to the dictates of an upright conscience).[9]

What is valid on the international level is equally true from the national point of view. Since the State must recognize the dignity of its citizens, as moral subjects, it must, therefore, also legally guarantee religious freedom.

The juridical proclamation of religious freedom must be all the more dear to Catholics as it is fully in accord with their doctrine on the act of faith, a free gift of God and a free engagement of man.

In order that the juridical expression of freedom of religion be real and efficacious, it is necessary that this personal right be subject only to indispensable restriction: as much freedom as possible. In other words, being a *moral subject*, the person must have the opportunity to assume the responsibility of the free acts which his conscience dictates to him in the religious domain. But the person is also a *social being*. In order to be faithful to what he is, he must, therefore, carry out his social obligations. It belongs to authority to enforce the social requirements and defend them; it has to impose, for that purpose, restrictions on the activities of those who, perhaps even in good faith, act contrary to the true social obligations. In the domain of religious freedom — as also in that of other rights and freedoms — Article 29, Section 2 of the *Universal Declaration of Human Rights* speaks of these restrictions: "In the exercise of his rights and freedoms, everyone shall be subject only to such limitations as are determined by law solely for the purpose of securing due recognition and respect for the rights and freedoms of others and of meeting the just requirements of morality, public order and the general welfare in a democratic society." This text manifestly coming from a generous intention, defines the restrictions in the exercise of personal rights by some expressions capable of putting in jeopardy these very rights. In fact, will not the interpretation that those who are in power give to it depend on their conception of morals, public order, the general good, and democracy? We prefer to say that the restrictions are attributable to the demands of the common good, that is, to the *requirements of coexistence, collaboration and coparticipation.* Indeed, these notions manifest more certainly a personalist sense. They place in a prominent position the fact that, in the last instance, every limitation on the exercise of personal rights can be imposed only for the purpose of benefiting the good of of the persons and of being useful to their dignity. It is a question, in fact, of the demands of *coexistence* of human persons as such, of the *collaboration* directed to the realization of values which are cultural, human and fruitful due to the diversity of the capacities of human persons, of the *coparticipation* in the benefits of collaboration in view of the subjective culture of each and every person. The common good, defined in this way, takes on an eminently personalist signification. Then, measures impairing the dignity of human person should never be able to be proposed because of the requirements of the common good. On the contrary, if the true demands of coexistence, collaboration or coparticipation place restrictions on the exercise of personal freedom, these restrictions will still be beneficial even to those which they impair: indeed, the promotion of coexistence, collaboration and coparticipation constitutes an integral part of their personal destiny as social beings. By living enclosed within himself, the person is not able to pursue his moral perfection; he is an open reality; it is only by developing the objective sense of his relations that he fulfills his appropriate completion as a human person. This openness includes, among other things, that he is a social being; then, the requirements of love and justice in coexistence, the acceptance of work as a social service in collaboration, the assent to the demands of distributive justice in coparticipation arise from his destiny and his personal perfection. When authority applies to the exercise of personal rights — therefore, to the right of freedom of conscience also — restrictions required by coexistence, collaboration and coparticipation, it is not encroaching upon the dignity of the person; on the contrary, it is defending and protecting it.

As for limitations in the domain of religious freedom, *they arise principally from the requirements of coexistence.* If, for example, the members of the predominant religious community hinder the religious freedom of other minority groups by forbidding them to preach in public, by forbidding them to hold gatherings for worship, by prohibiting them from places where they can meet together, etc., authority has the obligation of protecting the religious freedom of these minorities in the name of justice, an essential requirement of coexistence. Similarly, if one sect were practicing again human sacrifices or was starting a "holy war" for the purpose of destroying other religions, justice would require a determined intervention of authority with the aim of protecting basic human rights. Or again, when the members of one religious community indulge in forms of dishonest proselytism like restraint, calumny, invective, threats, etc., authority must impose penalties in order to protect the human values of coexistence.

In view of all that we have said, we come to the following conclusions: (1) considering that States and the international community are limited to the temporal domain, their authority is not competent to intervene directly in the religious domain as such: it can interfere in the domain of religious freedom only to enforce the demands of coexistence, collaboration and coparticipation; (2) since it must *respect* the dignity as moral subjects of those under its jurisdiction, it has a duty to guarantee the religious freedom of all; (3) since it must *enforce* respect by each person for the dignity as moral subjects of everyone, it has the obligation of imposing on the exercise of religious freedom the restrictions indispensable for this result; (4) in cases in which restrictions prove necessary, the interferences of authority will be based exclusively on the demands of the common temporal good — therefore, on the demands of coexistence, collaboration and coparticipation — and not on one or other particular religious conviction; moreover, these interventions will apply in an equal way to all members of the society without any distinction between religious convictions; (5) if the authority grants subsidies to organized groups on the basis of a religious conviction or a conception of life — this can be justified because these groups are making use of activities for teaching, education and moral formation in the service of the common good — the distribution of these subsidies must be made according to sociological criteria — proportionally with what different groups represent from the point of view of the number of members or the diversity of activities — and not according to a dogmatic discrimination based on a given preference for one or other conception.

Placing itself in the perspective of the common temporal good — the only thing which belongs to its competence — the authority of the States or the international community must treat all its subjects on an equal footing, whatever their religious convictions may be. But is this attitude still justified if one considers the problem of freedom of conscience from the point of view of the Church?

The Church and Temporal Societies

In the Old Testament Israel appears as the people of God. The legislation of Moses organized it as a true theocracy. God is the ruler of Israel and those who govern in His name assure the exercise of His sovereignty over the whole life of the nation in its religious aspects as well as its temporal. In fact, in its quality as the people of God Israel is sprung from a religious vocation, its national history is only the setting of its religious destiny, its civil legislation is directly for the benefit of its religious mission. It is, therefore, not surprising that the law of Moses punishes with the penalty of death offenses against the religious order, such as: blasphemy, idolatry, false prophecy, etc. It goes without saying that, in such a theocratic regime, the civil society has no autonomy and that it is only a means in the furtherance of religious interests.

Christ radically changed this situation. His Church, as it is described in the New Testament, has very new norms.

It is by taking into account these principles which Christ Himself communicated to His Church, that we have at our disposal the essential principles which govern the relations between the Church and temporal societies. In the light of these principles, do temporal societies perfectly respect the essence and the mission of the Church by guaranteeing, by a juridical statute and in an equal manner for all, the religious freedom of all their members?

1. The Church does not coincide with any nation. She addresses herself to all humanity by virtue of the universal mission which her divine Founder confided to her. In order to justify the dimension of this mission, the Church calls upon her universal sovereignty: "All power has been given to Me in heaven and on earth." The universality of the mission of the sole Mediator who gave Himself as a ransom for all mankind is carried on in the mission of the Church: "Go therefore.

Make disciples of all nations, baptizing them in the name of the Father and of the Son and of the Holy Spirit, teaching them to keep all that I have commanded you. And behold, I am with you all days, even to the end of the world" (Matt. 28:18-20). Whereas in the Old Testament the religious community called by God was identified with a particular people, Christ founded a universal Church whose religious mission is destined for people of all times. It follows that every attempt to reduce Christianity to the limits of a national Church contradicts the universal character of the institution of Christ. It follows again that no authority in temporal society can arrogate to itself the right to forbid its subjects to be part of the universal Church. Now, when the authority of temporal societies guarantees religious freedom in an equal way for all its subjects, it corresponds perfectly to the demands of the universal mission of the Church: by sanctioning freedom of conviction for all, it closes the door to any attempt to impose a national religion; it allows everyone full freedom to adhere to the Church.

2. Christ established decisive distinction between God and Caesar, between the spiritual authority of the Church and the temporal power of earthly societies: "Render therefore to Caesar the things which are Caesar's and to God the things that are God's" (Matt. 22:21). Leo XIII defined this distinction between the Church and civil society by saying that the Church has as its mission the obtaining of divine goods for us, while the State is concerned with human interests,[10] that the Church and civil society each have their own spheres, that each is sovereign in its own area and is not subject to the other in that particular domain: "Ecclesia et civitas suam habet utraque potestatem, neutra paret alteri." [11] Every confusion between the Church and temporal society and every intrusion by one in the domain belonging to the other is opposed to the real distinction between the earthly domain and the religious domain. Even if the whole population of a country is Catholic,

the State keeps temporal matters within its jurisdiction and the Church keeps spiritual matters, and the two are not fused into one theocracy as was the case in Old Testament times. Even if the union of States develops into a truly universal community, the latter remains confined to the temporal domain and, therefore, distinct from the universal Church. Temporal societies — States and international society — exercise in a sovereign way their competence in the domain of temporal values. Now, in order to meet the demands of justice in this domain, they must recognize the fundamental equality of all their members in their dignity as human persons. In other words, they have to promote temporal good in an identical way for all and assure the enjoyment of the same rights by all, no matter what their religious convictions may be. Confined to the temporal order, they are not qualified to set themselves up as judges in the religious domain. Consequently, they are not qualified to require that their members have faith or belong to a definite religion in order to be able to participate loyally, without restrictions and by right, in the life in society either on a national or international level. The confirmation of religious freedom by a juridical statute corresponds perfectly to their role and to their competence: by proclaiming religious freedom for all, they do not overstep the limits of the temporal domain which is suitable to them, and they grant to all their members, whatever may be their religious conviction, the same civil rights; this is an essential exigency of justice.

3. The Church has received from Our Lord a supernatural mission preserved from the jurisdiction of national or international temporal societies. In order to accomplish this mission Christ has confided to it means of action which are reserved to it and in no way displace temporal societies. He has conferred on it hierarchical powers by which, in His name and under the action of the Holy Spirit, it must enforce the demands of his revelation in the life of its faithful and assure their communion

with God by the sacred signs of His sacrificial and sacramental worship. Without being of the world (John 17:15; 18:36), it must be in the world, but with the means which are proper to it and which, in virtue of their supernatural essence transcend the temporal order. It proceeds from the fact that temporal societies must recognize their limits. That is why the state, for example, cannot be totalitarian, that is, it cannot claim to dictate the life and the whole destiny of its citizens. That would be secularism, the very negation of supernatural religion. By that very fact the State would abandon the temporal domain to which it belongs and would unduly usurp a competence for the solution of the religious problems of its citizens. To this secularism we oppose an "open secularity." What do we understand by this expression? By "secularity" we mean that the State must confine itself within the secular domain; by "open" we stress that its temporal institutions have to respect the religious domain. Now, once again, the juridical recognition of the religious freedom of all individuals and their groups is for temporal societies, national or international, the effective means of not overstepping the limits of their competence and of respecting the transcendency of the Church.

4. Each individual belongs necessarily to certain temporal societies. Participation in the life of the Church, on the contrary, is a free gift of God, and for those who are capable of committing themselves conscientiously and freely, adherence to the Church by an act of faith depends on their free consent. In order to respect the supernatural and free character of this adherence to the Church, temporal societies must allow their members to participate with complete freedom in the life of the Church. Temporal societies, on the national as well as on the international level, will meet this obligation by every juridical act which will proclaim and guarantee freedom of religion to all persons and to all groups.

1. L. Cerfaux, *Le Christ dans la theologie de saint Paul*, Paris, 1954, p. 54.

2. S. Augustin, *In Joh.*, tr. 26, 2 (PL, t. 33, col. 1607).

3. Saint Thomas is much more severe concerning heretics who have received the faith but who show resistance to it by violating it: *qui profitentur fidem Evangelii et ei renituntur, eam corrumpentes* (*Summa Theol.*, IIa-IIae, q. 10, art. 6). Restraint can be put on them, even corporal violence, in order to force them to remain faithful to what they have promised and to preserve the faith which they have received: *et tales sunt etiam corporaliter compellendi, ut impleant quod promiserunt et teneant quod semel susceperunt* (*ibid.*, art 8). Making a promise is an act of the will and keeping it is a necessity. That applies also to faith: *accipere fidem est voluntatis, sed tenere eam acceptam est necessitatis* (*ibid.*, art. 8. ad 3). If after repeated admonitions the heretic does not repent, the Church will excommunicate him and hand him over to the secular authority in order that he be punished by death. (*ibid.*, q. 11, art. 3, and 4). How can this attitude, which shocks us today, be explained? 1.) Explaining a passage of Saint. Augustine, Saint Thomas asserts that heresy is a free and conscious violation of a promise; *in bad faith*, especially with motives of greed and pride, the heretic does violence to the faith: *haereticus est qui alicuius temporalis commodi et maxime gloriae principatusque gratia, falsas ac novas opiniones vel gignit vel sequitur* (Augustine). The heretic is therefore acting in bad faith and he has his motives: *causa eius, sc. quod oritur* (haeresis) *ex superbia vel cupiditate* (*ibid.*, q. 11, art. 1, in corp. et ad 2 et 3). The outlook today is another matter. Who would dare to doubt the good faith and sincerity of our separated brethren and non-Christians? What must our attitude be in their regard? The answer will not be provided by Saint Thomas where he speaks in the same article of those who are acting in good faith — for him, those who do not yet possess the Christian faith — toward whom our attitude must consist in respecting their freedom since the act of faith is in its very essence a free act (*ibid.*, q. 10, art. 8). In defending religious freedom, we are only restating the principle which Saint Thomas speaks of here. It is in the area of *acts* that we separate ourselves from him. The fact of invincible and non-blameworthy error (good faith), which Saint Thomas does not agree to in the domain of faith—*omnis homo tenetur scire ea quae fidei sunt* (*De Malo*, q. 3, art. 7), appears very frequent to us since we are faced with separated brethren, non-Christian religions and atheists. 2.) Christianity of the Middle Ages was characterized by the mingling of the Church and civil society. Unity of faith was considered an important element for the common good of that theocratic community. That is why the secular power, in serving the common good, had to punish

heretics more severely than counterfeiters. The heretic was going against the spiritual unity of the community and, consequently, against an element of the common good which was much more important than material interest (*ibid.*, q. 11, art. 3). In our days we are sufficiently removed from that historical situation in order to give due recognition to the very clear distinction which Christ established between spiritual and temporal matters and to recognize the powers belonging to the Church and those belonging to temporal societies.

4. Pius XII, *Message of September 2, 1956 to the 77th Katholikentag.*

5. Pius XII, *Discourse of June 2, 1948 to the Sacred College.*

6. Pius XII, *Message of April 24, 1957 to the Congress of the Pax Romana.*

7. Cardinal Roncalli (John XXIII), Discourse of June 18, 1951 (UNESCO), in *Oss. Rom.* of June 29, 1951.

8. Pius XII, *Discourse of February 20, 1946 to the New Cardinals.*

9. Leo XIII, *Immortale Dei.*

10. On the subject of the universal Declaration of Human Rights, cf. A. Verdoodt, *Naissance et signification de la Déclaration Universelle des Drotits de l'Homme,* Louvain, 1964.

11. Leo XIII, *Sapientiae christianae.*

DECLARATION ON RELIGIOUS FREEDOM OF VATICAN COUNCIL II

Following, in a translation by the National Catholic Welfare Conference, endorsed by the Bishops of the United States, is the text of the Ecumenical Council's declaration on freedom of religion, which was promulgated December 7, 1965.

ON THE RIGHT OF THE PERSON AND OF COMMUNITIES TO SOCIAL AND CIVIL FREEDOM IN MATTERS RELIGIOUS

1

A sense of the dignity of the human person has been impressing itself more and more deeply on the consciousness of contemporary man, and the demand is increasingly made that men should act on their own judgment, enjoying and making use of a responsible freedom, not driven by coercion but motivated by a sense of duty. The demand is likewise made that constitutional limits should be set to the powers of government, in order that there may be no encroachment on the rightful freedom of the person and of associations.

This demand for freedom in human society chiefly regards the quest for the values proper to the human spirit. It regards, in the first place, the free exercise of religion in society. This Vatican Council takes careful note of these desires in the minds of men. It proposes to declare them to be greatly in accord with truth and justice. To this end, it searches into the sacred tradition and doctrine of the church—the treasury out of which the church continually brings forth new things that are in harmony with the things that are old.

First, the Council professes its belief that God himself has made known to mankind the way in which men are to serve him, and thus be saved in Christ and come to blessedness. We believe that this one true religion subsists in the Catholic and apostolic church, to which the Lord Jesus committed the duty of spreading it abroad among all men. Thus he spoke to the apostles: "Go, therefore, and make disciples of all nations, baptizing them in the name of the Father and of the Son and of the Holy Spirit, teaching them to observe all things whatsoever I have enjoined upon you" (Matthew XXVIII, 19-20).

On their part, all men are bound to seek the truth, especially in what concerns God and His church, and to embrace the truth they come to know, and to hold fast to it.

This Vatican Council likewise professes its belief that it is upon the human conscience that these obligations fall and exert their binding force. The truth cannot impose itself except by virtue of its own truth, as it makes its entrance into the mind at once quietly and with power.

Religious freedom, in turn, which men demand as necessary to fulfill their duty to worship God, has to do with immunity from coercion in civil society. Therefore it leaves untouched traditional Catholic doctrine on the moral duty of men and societies toward the true religion and toward the one church of Christ.

Over and above all this, the Council intends to develop the doctrine of recent Popes on the inviolable rights of the human person and the constitutional order of society.

GENERAL PRINCIPLES OF RELIGIOUS FREEDOM

2

This Vatican Council declares that the human person has a right to religious freedom. This freedom means that all men are to be immune from coercion on the part of individuals or of social groups and of any human power, in such ways that no one is to be forced to act in a manner contrary to his own beliefs, whether privately or publicly, whether alone or in association with others, within due limits.

The Council further declares that the right to religious freedom has its foundation in the very dignity of the human person as this dignity is known through the revealed word of God and by reason itself. This right of the human person to religious freedom is to be recognized in the constitutional law whereby society is governed and thus it is to become a civil right.

It is in accordance with their dignity as persons—that is, beings endowed with reason and free will and therefore privileged to bear personal responsibility—that all men should be at once impelled by nature and also bound by a moral obligation to seek the truth, especially religious truth. They are also bound to adhere to the truth, once it is known, and to order their whole lives in accord with the demands of truth.

However, men cannot discharge these obligations in a manner in keeping with their own nature unless they enjoy immunity from external coercion as well as psychological freedom. Therefore the right to religious freedom has its foundation, not in the subjective disposition of the person, but in his very nature. In consequence, the right to this immunity continues to exist even in those who do not live up to their obligation of seeking the truth and adhering to it and the exercise of this right is not to be impeded, provided that just public order be observed.

Further light is shed on the subject if one considers that the highest norm of human life is the divine law—eternal, objective, and universal—whereby God orders, directs, and governs the entire universe and all the ways of the human community, by a plan conceived in wisdom and love. Man has been made by God to participate in this law, with the result that, under a gentle disposition of divine Providence, he can come to perceive ever more fully the truth that is unchanging.

Wherefore every man has the duty, and therefore the right,

to seek the truth in matters religious, in order that he may with prudence form for himself right and true judgments of conscience, under use of all suitable means.

Truth, however, is to be sought after in a manner proper to the dignity of the human person and his social nature. The inquiry is to be free, carried on with the aid of teaching or instruction, communication and dialogue, in the course of which men explain to one another the truth they have discovered, or think they have discovered, in order thus to assist one another in the quest for truth.

Moreover, as the truth is discovered, it is by a personal assent that men are to adhere to it.

3

On his part, man perceives and acknowledges the imperatives of the divine law through the mediation of conscience. In all his activity a man is bound to follow his conscience in order that he may come to God, the end and purpose of life. It follows that he is not to be forced to act in a manner contrary to his conscience.

Nor on the other hand, is he to be restrained from acting in accordance with his conscience, especially in matters religious. The reason is that the exercise of religion, of its very nature, consists before all else in those internal, voluntary, and free acts whereby man sets the course of his life directly toward God. No merely human power can either command or prohibit acts of this kind.

The social nature of man, however, itself requires that he should give external expression to his internal acts of religion: that he should share with others in matters religious: that he should profess his religion in community. Injury therefore is done to the human person and to the very order established by God for human life, if the free exercise of religion is denied in society, provided just public order is observed.

There is a further consideration. The religious acts whereby men, in private and in public and out of a sense of personal conviction, direct their lives to God transcend by their very nature the order of terrestrial and temporal affairs.

Government, therefore, ought indeed to take account of the religious life of the citizenry and show it favor, since the function of government is to make provision for the common welfare. However, it would clearly transgress the limits set to its power, were it to presume to command or inhibit acts that are religious.

4

The freedom or immunity from coercion in matters religious which is the endowment of persons as individuals is also to be recognized as their right when they act in community. Religious communities are a requirement of the social nature both of man and of religion itself.

Provided the just demands of public order are observed, religious communities rightfully claim freedom in order that they may govern themselves according to their own norms, honor the Supreme Being in public worship, assist their members in the practice of the religious life, strengthen them by instruction, and promote institutions in which they may join together for the purpose of ordering their own lives in accordance with their religious principles.

Religious communities also have the right not to be hindered, either by legal measures or by administrative action on the part of the government, in the selection, training, appointment, and transferral of their own ministers in communicating with religious authorities and communities abroad in erecting buildings for religious purposes, and in the acquisition and use of suitable funds or properties.

Religious communities also have the right not to be hindered in their public teaching and witness to their faith, whether by the spoken or by the written word. However, in spreading religious faith and in introducing religious practices everyone ought at all times to refrain from any manner of action which might seem to carry a hint of coercion or of a kind of persuasion that would be dishonorable or unworthy, especially when dealing with poor or uneducated people. Such a manner of action would have to be considered an abuse of one's right and a violation of the right of others.

In addition, it comes within the meaning of religious freedom that religious communities should not be prohibited from freely undertaking to show the special value of their doctrine in what concerns the organization of society and the inspiration of the whole of human activity.

Finally, the solid nature of man and the very nature of religion afford the foundation of the right of men freely to hold meetings and to establish educational, cultural, charitable and social organizations, under the impulse of their own religious sense.

5

The family, since it is a society in its own original right, has the right freely to live its own domestic religious life under the guidance of parents. Parents, moreover, have the right to determine, in accordance with their own religious beliefs, the kind of religious education that their children are to receive.

Government, in consequence, must acknowledge the right of parents to make a genuinely free choice of schools and of other means of education, and the use of this freedom of choice is not to be made a reason for imposing unjust burdens on parents, whether directly or indirectly.

Besides, the rights of parents are violated if their children are forced to attend lessons or instruction which are not in agreement with their religious beliefs, or if a single system of education, from which all religious information is excluded, is imposed upon all.

6

Since the common welfare of society consists in the entirety of those conditions of social life under which men enjoy the possibility of achieving their own perfection in a certain fullness of measure and also with some relative ease, it chiefly consists in the protection of the rights, and in the performance of the duties, of the human person.

Therefore the care of the right to religious freedom devolves upon the whole citizenry, upon social groups, upon government, and upon the church and other religious communities, in virtue of the duty of all toward the common welfare, and in the manner proper to each.

The protection and promotion of the inviolable rights of man ranks among the essential duties of government. Therefore government is to assume the safeguard of the religious freedom of all its citizens, in an effective manner, by just laws and by other appropriate means.

Government is also to help create conditions favorable to the fostering of religious life, in order that the people may be truly enabled to exercise their religious rights and to fulfill their religious duties, and also in order that society itself may profit by the moral qualities of justice and peace which have their origin in men's faithfulness to God and to His holy will.

If, in view of peculiar circumstances obtaining among peoples, special civil recognition is given to one religious community in the constitutional order of society, it is at the same time imperative that the right of all citizens and religious communities to religious freedom should be recognized and made effective in practice.

Finally, government is to see to it that the equality of citizens before the law, which is itself an element of the common good, is never violated, whether openly or covertly, for religious reasons. Nor is there to be discrimination among citizens.

It follows that a wrong is done when government imposes upon its people, by force or fear or other means, the profession or repudiation of any religion, or when it hinders men from joining or leaving a religious community. All the more is it a violation of the will of God and of the sacred rights of the person and the family of nations, when force is brought to bear in any way in order to destroy or repress religion, either in the whole of mankind or in a particular country or in a definite community.

7

The right to religious freedom is exercised in human society: hence its exercise is subject to certain regulatory norms. In the use of all freedoms the moral principle of personal and social responsibility is to be observed. In the exercise of their rights individual men and social groups are bound by the moral law to have respect both for the rights of others and for their own duties toward others and for the common welfare of all. Men are to deal with their fellows in justice and civility. Furthermore, society has the right to defend itself against possible abuses committed on pretext of freedom of religion. It is the special duty of government to provide this protection. However, government is not to act in arbitrary fashion or in an unfair spirit of partisanship. Its action is to be controlled by juridical norms which are in conformity with the objective moral order.

These norms arise out of the need for effective safeguard of the rights of all citizens and for peaceful settlement of conflicts of rights, also out of the need for an adequate care of genuine public peace, which comes about when men live together in good order and in true justice: and finally out of the need for a proper guardianship of public morality.

These matters constitute the basic component of the common welfare: they are what is meant by public order. For the rest, the usages of society are to be the usages of freedom in their full range: that is, the freedom of man is to be respected as far as possible and is not to be curtailed except when and insofar as necessary.

8

Many pressures are brought to bear upon men of our day, to the point where the danger arises lest they lose the possibility of acting on their own judgment. On the other hand, not a few can be found who seem inclined to use the name of freedom as the pretext for refusing to submit to authority and for making light of the duty of obedience.

Wherefore this Vatican Council urges everyone, especially those who are charged with the task of educating others, to do their utmost to form men who, on the other hand, will respect the moral order and be obedient to lawful authority, and, on the other hand, will be lovers of true freedom—men, in other words, who will come to decisions on their own judgment and in the light of truth, govern their activities with a sense of responsibility, and strive after what is true and right, willing always to join with others in cooperative effort.

Religious freedom therefore ought to have this further purpose and aim, namely, that men may come to act with greater responsibility in fulfilling their duties in community life.

RELIGIOUS FREEDOM IN THE LIGHT OF REVELATION

9

The declaration of this Vatican Council on the right of man to religious freedom has its foundation in the dignity of the person, whose exigencies have come to be more fully known to human reason through centuries of experience. What is more, this doctrine of freedom has roots in divine revelation, and for this reason Christians are bound to respect it all the more conscientiously.

Revelation does not indeed affirm in so many words the right of man to immunity from external coercion in matters religious. It does, however, disclose the dignity of the human person in its full dimensions: it gives evidence of the respect which Christ showed toward the freedom with which man is to fulfill his duty of belief in the word of God: and it gives us lessons in the spirit which disciples of such a master ought to adopt and continually follow.

Thus further light is cast upon the general principles upon which the doctrine of this declaration on religious freedom is based. In particular, religious freedom in society is entirely consonant with the freedom of the act of Christian faith.

10

It is one of the major tenets of Catholic doctrine that man's response to God in faith must be free: no one therefore is to be forced to embrace the Christian faith against his own will. This doctrine is contained in the word of God and it was constantly proclaimed by the fathers of the church. The act of faith is of its very nature a free act. Man, redeemed by Christ the Savior and through Christ Jesus called to be God's adopted son, cannot give his adherence to God revealing Himself unless, under the drawing of the Father he offers to God the reasonable and free submission of faith.

It is therefore completely in accord with the nature of faith that in matters religious every manner of coercion on the part of men should be excluded. In consequence, the principle of religious freedom makes no small contribution to the creation of an environment in which men can without hindrance be invited to Christian faith, embrace it of their own free will, and profess it effectviely in their whole manner of life.

11

God calls men to serve Him in spirit and in truth: hence they are bound in conscience but they stand under no compulsion. God has regard for the dignity of the human person whom He Himself created: man is to be guided by his own judgment and he is to enjoy freedom.

This truth appears at its height in Christ Jesus, in whom God manifested Himself and His ways with men. Christ is at once our Master and our Lord and also meek and humble of heart: in attracting and inviting His disciples He used patience. He wrought miracles to illuminate His teaching and to establish its truth: but His intention was to rouse faith in His hearers and to confirm them in faith, not to exert coercion upon them. He did indeed denounce the unbelief of some who listened to Him, but He left vengeance to God in expectation of the day of judgment.

When He sent His apostles into the world, He said to them: "He who believes and is baptized will be saved: he who does not believe will be condemned" (Mark, XVI, 16). But He himself, noting that cockle had been sown amid the wheat, gave orders that both should be allowed to grow until the harvest time, which will come at the end of the world. He refused to be a political messiah, ruling by force; He preferred to call Himself the son of man, who came "to serve and to give his life as a ransom for the many" (Mark X, 45). He showed Himself the perfect servant of God, who "does not break the bruised reed nor extinguish the smoking flax" (Matthew XII, 20).

He acknowledged the power of government and its rights, when He commanded that tribute be given to Caesar: but He gave clear warning that the higher rights of God are to be kept inviolate: "Render to Caesar the things that are Caesar's and to God the things that are God's" (Matthew, XXII, 21).

In the end when He completed on the cross the work of redemption whereby He achieved salvation and true freedom for men, He brought His revelation to completion. For He bore witness to the truth, but He refused to impose the truth by force on those who spoke against it. Not by force of blows does His rule assert its claims. It is established by witnessing to the truth and by hearing the truth, and it extends its dominion by the love whereby Christ, lifted up on the cross, draws all men to Himself.

Taught by the word and example of Christ, the apostles followed the same way. From the very origins of the church the disciples of Christ strove to convert men to faith in Christ as the Lord—not, however, by the use of coercion or devices unworthy of the gospel, but by the power, above all, of the word of God, steadfastly they proclaimed to all the plan of God our Savior, "who wills that all men should be saved and come to the acknowledgement of the truth" (I Timothy, II, 4).

At the same time, however, they showed respect for those of weaker stuff, even though they were in error, and thus they made it plain that "each one of us is to render to God an account of himself" (Romans XIV, 12), and for that reason is bound to obey his conscience. Like Christ himself, the apostles were unceasingly bent upon bearing witness to the truth of God, and they showed the fullest measure of boldness in "speaking of the word with confidence" (Acts IV, 31) before the people and their rulers.

With a firm faith they held that the gospel is indeed the power of God unto salvation for all who believe. Therefore they rejected all carnal weapons. They followed the example of the gentleness and respectfulness of Christ and they preached the word of God in the full confidence that there was resident in this word itself a divine power able to destroy all the forces arrayed against God and bring men to faith in Christ and to his service.

As the Master, so too the apostles recognized legitimate civil authority. For there is no power except from God, the apostle teaches, and thereafter commands: "Let everyone be subject to higher authorities . . . : He who resists authority resists God's ordinance" (Romans XIII, 1-5). At the same time, however, they did not hesitate to speak out against governing powers which set themselves in opposition to the holy will of God: "It is necessary to obey God rather than men" (Acts V, 29). This is the way along which the martyrs and other faithful have walked through all ages and over all the earth.

12

In faithfulness therefore to the truth of the gospel, the church is following the way of Christ and the apostles when she recognizes, and gives support to the principle of religious freedom as befitting the dignity of man and as being in accord with divine revelation.

Throughout the ages the church has kept safe and handed on the doctrine received from the Master and from the apostles. In the life of the people of God as it has made its pilgrim way through the vicissitudes of human history, there has at times appeared a way of acting that was hardly in accord with the spirit of the gospel or even opposed to it. Nevertheless, the doctrine of the church that no one is to be coerced into faith has always stood firm.

Thus the leaven of the gospel has long been about its quiet work in the minds of men, and to it is due in great measure the fact that in the course of time men have come more widely to recognize their dignity as persons, and the conviction has grown stronger that the person in society is to be kept free from all manner of coercion in matters religious.

13

Among the things that concern the good of the church and indeed the welfare of society here on earth—things therefore that are always and everywhere to be kept secure and defended against all injury—this certainly is pre-eminent, namely, that the church should enjoy that full measure of freedom which her care for the salvation of men requires.

This is a sacred freedom, because the only-begotten son endowed with it the church which He purchased with His blood. Indeed it is so much the property of the church that to act against it is to act against the will of God. The freedom of the church is the fundamental principle in what concerns the relations between the church and governments and the whole civil order.

In human society and the face of government the church claims freedom for herself in her character as a spiritual authority, established by Christ the Lord, upon which there rests, by divine mandate, the duty of going out into the whole world and preaching the gospel to every creature. The church also claims freedom for herself in her character as a society of men who have the right to live in society in accordance with the precepts of Christian faith.

In turn, where the principle of religious freedom is not only proclaimed in words or simply incorporated in law but also given sincere and practical application, there the church succeeds in achieving a stable situation of right as well as of fact and the independence which is necessary for the fulfillment of her divine mission.

This independence is precisely what the authorities of the church claim in society. At the same time, the Christian faithful, in common with all other men, possess the civil right not to be hindered in leading their lives in accordance with their conscience. Therefore a harmony exists between the freedom of the church and the religious freedom which is to be recognized as the right of all men and communities and sanctioned by constitutional law.

14

In order to be faithful to the divine command, "teach all nations" (Matthew XXVIII, 19-20), the Catholic Church must work with all urgency and concern "that the word of God be spread abroad and glorified" (II Thessalonians III, 1). Hence the church earnestly begs of its children that, "first of all, supplications, prayers, petitions, acts of thanksgiving be made for all men . . . . For this is good and agreeable in the sight of God our Savior, who wills that all men be saved and come to the knowledge of the truth" (I Timothy II, 1-4).

In the formation of their consciences the Christian faithful ought carefully to attend to the sacred and certain doctrine of the church. For the church is, by the will of Christ, the teacher of the truth. It is her duty to give utterance to, and authoritatively to teach that truth which is Christ Himself, and also, to declare and confirm by her authority those principles of the moral order which have their origin in human nature itself.

Furthermore, let Christians walk in wisdom in the face of

those outside, "in the Holy Spirit in unaffected love, in the word of truth" (II Corinthians VI, 6-7), and let them be about their task of spreading the light of life with all confidence and apostolic courage, even to the shedding of their blood.

The disciple is bound by a grave obligation toward Christ his Master ever more fully to understand the truth received from Him, faithfully to proclaim it, and vigorously to defend it, never—be it understood—having recourse to means that are incompatible with the spirit of the Gospel.

At the same time, the charity of Christ urges him to love and have prudence and patience in his dealings with those who are in error or in ignorance with regard to the faith. All is to be taken into account—the Christian duty to Christ, the life-giving word which must be proclaimed, and the rights of the human person, and the measure of grace granted by God through Christ to men, who are invited freely to accept and profess the faith.

15

The fact is that men of the present day want to be able freely to profess their religion in private and public; indeed religious freedom has already been declared to be a civil right in most constitutions and it is solemnly recognized in international documents. The further fact is that forms of government still exist under which, even though freedom of religious worship receives constitutional recognition, the powers of government are engaged in the effort to deter citizens from the profession of religion and to make life very difficult and dangerous for religious communities.

This Council greets with joy the first of these two facts, as among the signs of the times. With sorrow, however, it denounces the other fact, as only to be deplored. The Council exhorts Catholics, and it directs a plea to all men, most carefully to consider how greatly necessary religious freedom is, especially in the present condition of the human family.

All nations are coming into even closer unity: men of different cultures and religions are being brought together in closer relationships: there is a growing consciousness of the personal responsibility that every man has. All this is evident. Consequently, in order that relationships of peace and harmony be established and maintained within the whole of mankind, it is necessary that religious freedom be everywhere provided with an effective constitutional guarantee and that respect be shown for the high duty and right of man freely to lead his religious life in society.

May the God and Father of all grant that the human family, through careful observance of the principle of religious freedom in society, may be brought by the grace of Christ and the power of the Holy Spirit to the sublime and unending and "glorious freedom of the sons of God" (Romans VIII, 21).